WHY YOUR FATHER'S A REPUBLICAN
... AND YOU SHOULD BE TOO!

J. ALAN WILLIAMS

PELICAN BAY PRESS

ISBN-13: 978-0615846330 (Pelican Bay Press)

ISBN-10: 0615846335

Published in the United States of America

PELICAN BAY PRESS
P.O. BOX 724793
ATLANTA, GEORGIA 31139

WHY YOUR FATHER'S A REPUBLICAN
... AND YOU SHOULD BE TOO!

CONTENTS

AUTHOR'S NOTE

To the Parents:

Many of you may be wondering how to explain and educate your teen aged children about the ever present world of politics we now live in. Specifically, Democrat vs. Republican, Liberal vs. Conservative.

Even though they really don't seem interested, like me, you may have wondered what effect the barrage of misinformation coming from news outlets and a variety of other sources may be having on the formation of what will become their political ideology.

For the most part our children spend the entire school day being taught by liberal leaning educators. We want them to believe what they are taught about math and science but do we want them to believe revisionist history or slanted beliefs on social justice?

As a parent you may overhear things like little Suzy saying "I think they should make old man Edwards sell his farm to the city so our entire community can benefit from the new park and civic center" or your son says "I like Mayor Reed, he wants to stop pollution, save our environment, and keep our water clean. Vote for him Dad."

You may be tempted to stop and take the time to explain the differences between "eminent domain" and an individual's property rights, or delve into how politicians of all persuasions pander to their target audience while advocating universally accepted positions. Ultimately, you decide, they'll figure it out in time on their own, but will they?

After all, don't we all start out as liberals? We are all taught at an early age, to share, don't be stingy or greedy, and that if we don't bother our neighbor, our neighbor won't bother us. Peace is good, war is bad, can't we all just get along? It all seems so easy, so simplistic, just as it sounds in the John Lennon song *Imagine*.

There is a maturation process we all go through in the formation and development of our political beliefs. Today our kids are exposed to more sources of information than we could have ever dreamed... but are these sources balanced? Having more sources of information, is not a bad thing, but where is this information coming from, and is it factual?

Young and often naive minds are thirsting for knowledge but there are no guarantees that the presenters of this "knowledge" will be fair, balanced, or even factually correct. We live in a day and age where biases run rampant, from the news media, to the teachers in our children's classrooms.

Some are taught to believe the Robin Hood syndrome; rich people are bad and if not for the unfair practices of the rich, we would all be wealthy. Therefore, our mission in life should be to redistribute the wealth back to the rightful owners...everyone!

Or, maybe the Teddy Kennedy syndrome. Some people truly are fortunate enough to have been born into money, or have otherwise acquired it through no effort or actions of their own. They then feel compelled by their, for lack of a better word, guilt, to champion the cause of the "common man" and "give back to society," to right all of the wrongs caused by a capitalistic system. This helps them sleep at night. The problem is some are not satisfied with merely giving their money, they want the government to enact laws, forcing you to contribute your hard earned money to their causes. They are giving their money, why shouldn't you give yours?

Yes, most of us do start out as liberals, but as we mature and begin to collect real world experiences, this begins to change. Winston Churchill once said "If a man is twenty and not a liberal, he has no heart, if he is forty and not a conservative, he has no brain."

So how do you explain to your teenagers that things are not always as they appear? Just because someone looks them in the eye and tells them something is true, does not make it so. Furthermore, just because their teacher, a textbook, or the man on the six o'clock news says it's true, does not make it so. How many times have you heard your child say "It's on the internet, it must be true?"

In this book we will explore the history of the two parties, what each purports to stand for (and what their actions actually show). We will look at how so many commonly held beliefs in today's society are factually incorrect, while being taught and reported that way on purpose. My primary goal is to set forth the principles of what a *true* conservative is, to correct many of the misconceptions of "historical fact," and to illustrate to the next generation how easily one can become misinformed.

To the Students:

Do you ever wonder why your parents endorse a political candidate different from the one your teachers advocate, different from the ones some of your friends' parents support? Do you ever find yourself agreeing with your teacher's selection over that of your parents? Maybe you watch the evening news and wonder why your parents seem to be so against the generally accepted "mainstream" views? Or, do you adopt the views of your parents as your own, simply because it's what they believe?

When forming opinions or making decisions we are all limited by the source and amount of information we have in order to come to a conclusion. The purpose of this book is not necessarily to convince you to become a Republican. Its purpose is more to help you understand the key differences between the two prevailing political parties in America today. To understand the two totally different philosophies, and to provide some semblance of credible historical information upon which you can base your own political philosophy. You can decide for yourself whether your own personal philosophy tends to be more liberal or more conservative.

After all declaring yourself a Republican without understanding what that means, without knowing what that represents and stands for, would be the same as declaring yourself a Christian without understanding the core beliefs that are held by that religion.

Sadly, many people in our country do both, they choose their religious affiliation and their political affiliation based solely on what others in their demographic group think, or they choose whatever affiliation their parents have made, or even worse, they do make a conscious decision to choose, but the information they utilize to make this decision is flawed or incorrect.

As a teenager, you are probably interested in a myriad of different things: music, movies, sports, video games, computers and a lot more. The least likely subject matter you may be interested in is probably politics. This makes you a normal teen.

Still, you can't help but recognize differences in how people express opinions about different political candidates and parties. You may notice that family members' opinions differ from each other. During election years, you may see that your parents are in favor of a candidate that your neighbor is opposed to.

I've written this text in order to fill in some of the information that is left out of your school text books. In most cases, it would simply be impossible to include all of this information, in other cases there is a concerted effort to omit or revise historical fact.

Additionally, you must always be aware that every source from which you get your information is, or can be, biased. As you grow older, it becomes easier to filter incoming information through facts and understandings that you already know to be true. The problem when you're young is that you do not have these life experiences or first-hand accounts in order to help you gauge whether what a person says is consistent with what you already know to be true.

From the time you are in grade school (when we are all liberals!), through high school, and then particularly in college, you will be taught, instructed, and mentored by individuals who almost exclusively are proponents of the liberal mindset. This taints your information source. Many of these teachers realize they have an agenda, but many do not. They went to school and pursued a liberal arts or an education degree and from that point forward they were instilled with the mindset that their income is dependent upon public government funding. The government provides the building for you to go to school in, the lunch that you eat, the school buses that pick you up and return you home safely, the school books that you learn from... and your teachers' paychecks.

Do you see any opportunity for, or the possibility of, there being a distinct bias toward the mindset that the government will take care of all of your needs, therefore relieving you of the responsibility, or the opportunity, to take care of yourself?

While still denied by some, media bias is blatant in our country. Journalists went to the same liberal arts colleges that your teachers went to and may not have had the opportunity to grow and evolve past the classic liberal utopian mindset.

Journalists are not necessarily purposely biased, they suffer from what is called "group think." They all went to the same schools; they all work together, live in the same areas and socialize together. There is just not a lot of opportunity for independent thought. Consequently, many of them do not even realize they are injecting a bias into their reporting; others most definitely are seeking to advance a liberal agenda.

There are many teachers out there that are conservatives, and there are some conservative journalists as well, but generally speaking it has been well documented that the majority of educators and those in the mainstream media predominantly vote Democratic.

Biased does not necessarily mean wrong, a person can be biased and be 100% correct. I am biased in presenting the information contained in this book to you. My bias is based on over forty years of observing the media and the political parties from my perspective. While very difficult to achieve, some sources should strive to remain unbiased: those whose job it is to teach you, especially history and other societal viewpoints, and those whose job it is to report to you the news of the day. All you need to know are the facts: what occurred, and to whom. It's up to you to then decide why something may have occurred and what you may think about it.

After reading this book, it is my hope that you will be better informed to make your own decisions and choices as to which political philosophy best aligns with what you believe.

WHY YOUR FATHER'S A REPUBLICAN

CHAPTER ONE

MISCONCEPTIONS AND REVISIONIST HISTORY

"It's not that our liberal friends are ignorant, it's that they know so much that isn't so" - Ronald Reagan

Two philosophical adages come to mind as I present this chapter:

"Those who do not learn from history are doomed to repeat it" and "if you repeat a lie often enough, it will become truth."

In today's liberal society the Democratic Party is seen as the champion of the "working class" and the primary proponent of blacks and other minorities. There are two very good reasons for this belief.

One, the Democrats want you to believe this and routinely give speeches telling you this. According to them, if not for the Democratic Party, the working class would be far worse off than they are today, and no one would have stood up for the rights of blacks and other minorities in this country.

Two, most people don't know the history of our country. They may think they do, but they don't.

Consider this...

The Republican Party was formed in 1854 at a meeting in a small school house in Ripon, Wisconsin by a group of former Democrats who opposed slavery.

The Republican Party is often referred to as the party of Lincoln, Abraham Lincoln, the President in 1863 that signed the Emancipation Proclamation to end slavery.

Democrats Jefferson Davis, the President of the Confederacy and Alexander Stevens, Vice-President of the Confederacy led the fight to continue slavery in the South.

Lincoln, the first Republican President urged the mostly Republican 39th Congress to pass the 13th Amendment which outlawed slavery. Lincoln signed the legislation even though he didn't have to, because Congress sent it to the states for ratification which occurred on December 6, 1865.

Conversely, Thomas Jefferson, a co-founder of the Democratic Party and its first President, tried to legitimize slavery by having it written into the Constitution. The *true* conservatives of the time would not permit it. It is estimated that Mr. Jefferson owned over two hundred slaves in his lifetime. I do not wish to demonize President Jefferson, he was a great man and a great thinker, it was simply a different place and time. Jefferson's position on slavery is presented only to illustrate factual historical differences between the two parties.

Democrats, in retaliation for the reconstruction efforts of the North that were seen as forcing "northerner ways" upon the South after the Civil War organized groups like the Ku Klux Klan to terrorize black people who "did not know their place" and put into practice segregation which lasted into the 1960's in an effort to continue to oppress black people.

During the early 1960's, the movement to pass civil rights legislation was promoted by Republicans while ardently combated by southern Democrats. It was not until after President Kennedy's (D) death, when his successor Lyndon B. Johnson (D) had a (political) change of heart.

Question: Which political party was Dr. Martin Luther King, Jr. a member of for most of his life?
Answer: Dr. King was a registered member of the Republican Party, just as his father was.

(Dr. King was not a right-wing conservative by any means. My point is I'll bet you've never heard, or read, that he was a member of the Republican Party.)

Today, Democrats would have you believe that they alone championed landmark legislation like the 1964 Civil Rights Act, but that could not be further from the truth. President Johnson had not been a supporter of this legislation previously, but was facing his first election for the presidency in November 1964.

Johnson had a problem. Southern Democrats were not going to vote in favor of the bill. Robert Byrd, Democratic Senator from West Virginia, led a filibuster against the bill. (Byrd is also remembered for having been a member of the KKK.) In the end, President Johnson went to Republican Senator Everett Dirksen of Illinois who lined up enough Republican votes to pass the bill. This is how the 1964 Civil Rights Act became the law of the land.

The Voting Rights Act of 1965 had to be passed specifically because southern Democrats had enacted *Jim Crow* laws in order to prevent many black Americans from exercising their right to vote. The right of black Americans to vote was affirmed by the 15th Amendment to the U.S. Constitution, which was ratified in 1870. Yet today many Americans believe that black people could not vote until the mid-1960's. Furthermore, they are told that it was the Democratic Party that fought to deliver them this right. Historical fact shows otherwise.

Democrats like to portray Republicans as "old racist white men." Two of their favorite examples are former Senators Strom Thurmond from South Carolina and Jesse Helms from North Carolina. What they don't tell you is that through the civil rights movement of the 1950's and early 1960's these two were Democrats.

Affirmative Action, the process of combating racial discrimination in the workplace against one segment of the population by actively practicing racial discrimination against another segment, was greatly expanded during the Richard Nixon (R) administration.

Ronald Reagan, a Republican, was the President that declared Martin Luther King Jr's birthday a national holiday after son of the south, Democrat Jimmy Carter, was perennially asked, and perennially declined to do so, during his preceding four years as President.

Despite all of these facts, the majority of black people in this country oppose the "Party of Lincoln" and some possess an outright hatred for members of the Republican Party. I don't know of any other explanation for this other than they must be either misinformed or uninformed. This leads to the teaching of a key principle that will serve you well in all aspects of your life going forward; just because someone tells you something is true, does not make it so. They may be intentionally lying to you, may be mistaken, or have simply taken the word of others. Please know that it is incredibly difficult to reach the correct conclusion when you do not have the correct information on which to base an opinion.

In later chapters we will explore other reasons why many black Americans have gravitated to the Democratic Party but among them is certainly the fact that history has been "revised" and then repeated over and over again.

Other misconceptions we will discuss include the assertion that Republicans are against Latino or Hispanic immigrants coming into our country. Of course this is not true, we are a nation of immigrants, the debate has always been over *illegal immigration* and adherence to the rule of law that *all* Americans and *all* visitors to our country, should obey. The illegal immigration debate is more important than ever after the events of 9/11/2001 showed us how vulnerable our country is to attack from those who wish to do us harm. The reality is that Ronald Reagan, a

Republican, is the only American President who has ever granted amnesty to millions of illegal immigrants already in our country.

Obviously, it's not easy to know the truth about what happened two hundred or even one hundred years ago. Just remember to keep an open mind and make every attempt to gather your information from multiple sources. Just because it's broadcast on our national news, or appears on the internet as news, does not make it true. Unfortunately, the media is complicit in the diversion of truth, and in the revision of history, and it's not just history from centuries or decades ago.

Starting shortly after he left office in January 2001 and continuing today, President William Jefferson (Bill) Clinton (D) is commonly held up as an elder statesman of the Democratic Party. To this day, he is revered among the Hollywood elite and referred to often by many on the left when seeking to present an example of a truly fine President.

In reality, Mr. Clinton presided over a very chaotic time during his eight years in office. Much of this chaos was brought on by self-inflicted scandals that ran from the time he took office to the time he left.

Among liberals, it is a popular belief that Mr. Clinton ignited our economy when he came into office. History and statistical data show us that the tax increase Mr. Clinton pushed through Congress in 1993 actually served to slow what had been a strengthening economy coming out of the 1990-91 recession. Partially as a result of this tax policy, in 1994 the Republicans won back both houses of Congress taking a majority in the House of Representatives for the first time in forty years. The subsequent 1997 Republican led tax cuts, which created huge capital investment in our economy, as well as the exploding internet revolution are what led to our country's tremendous economic expansion in the late 1990's.

During Mr. Clinton's presidency our country was attacked four times* by Muslim terrorists (once on our own soil) and our country offered no meaningful response. This failure to adequately respond could have quite possibly contributed to the attack against us on 9/11/2001.

Mr. Clinton left office with our country in a recession that began during his last quarter and was passed onto President George W. Bush.

Mr. Clinton was the first President to have Articles of Impeachment filed against him by Congress since Andrew Johnson in 1868. He was acquitted at the impeachment hearing but later found to be in contempt of court for committing perjury (lying under oath) before a federal grand jury and was subsequently disbarred (losing his license to practice law.)

In history, things are not always as you may have been told.

*1993 World Trade Center Bombing
  1996 Khobar Tower Bombing
  1998 Two U.S. Embassies in Africa Bombed
  2000 U.S.S. Cole Bombing

CHAPTER TWO

WHAT IT MEANS TO BE A TRUE CONSERVATIVE

"The smallest minority on earth is the individual. Those who deny individual rights cannot claim to be defenders of minorities" - Ayn Rand

Just as in the past, being a conservative today means you want a smaller and less intrusive government than we currently have. It means that you recognize our government does not have a revenue problem, it has a spending problem. Cutting spending, rather than raising taxes in order to balance our budget and pay off the national debt should be our number one domestic concern.

As conservatives, we believe in the rights of individuals and are committed to maintaining a government that will not only lend support to, but also refrain from interference with all of our individual rights to pursue liberty and happiness.

In order to be a *true* conservative you must acknowledge and advocate for all of the rights and freedoms bestowed upon us by God as they are written in the United States Constitution.

As a *true* conservative, you cannot believe in dictating which religion a person can or cannot believe in, seek to dictate or control the rights an individual has over their own body, discriminate over a person's (legal) sexual preference in society, or discriminate against anyone based on their sex, race, color, or national origin.

A *true* conservative believes in the embodiment of the United States Constitution, that all people are created equal. The conservative party is the party of individual rights; we don't see people as a member of a group, but as individuals.

For these reasons, a *true* conservative can never be a racist. This is a point that we need to drive home. If you read this book in its entirety you will see how the Republican Party was formed with the fundamental belief that all people are created equal and possess the same inalienable rights. From Abraham Lincoln on, the Republican Party has represented the rights and freedoms of the individual, all individuals. It was only with the massive redistribution of wealth through government social welfare programs, that beginning in the 1960's, black Americans began voting primarily Democratic. They continue to do so to this day, some with the mindset that they need a "hand out" rather than a "hand up," many with the mistaken viewpoint that it has been the Republicans that have actively worked to keep them constrained. We need to change this belief by using historical and present day facts.

True conservatives understand that our country is not a true democracy; rather we are a constitutional republic, just as the pledge of allegiance refers to. A true democracy is majority rule. This could also be described as "mob" rule. You will hear it said that we are a nation of laws, not people. This is because people are fallible; they can, and do make mistakes. Laws are our rules for fairness. Just because a *majority* of the people on hand may not like you, then decide to hit you over the head and take your money, doesn't make it permissible. We have the rule of law to punish them if they do so.

True conservatives understand that it's not the speech that you agree with that needs to be protected, it's the speech you don't agree with. If you pay attention, you will see many examples of outspoken groups using the right to free speech to make their positions heard. These same groups will then try to shout down those who don't agree with them, and will often seek to have these individuals removed from their positions because they chose to voice their views and opinions. Some people don't understand that free speech is a two way street. The best example I can think of to illustrate this point is the burning of the American flag, an act that I hope seems abhorrent to you. So many of our countrymen have fought and died under our flag to protect our freedoms. Even so, it has been held up as constitutional that the burning of our flag is a permissible act under our freedom of expression rights. Even though I deem this act to be heinous, I must stand to protect the individual's right to do this if they choose to. What would freedom of speech mean otherwise? This position is very difficult for many to understand but I hope it clarifies the point that speech or expression, you agree with does not need to be protected. It's the speech you do not agree with that does.

A *true* conservative understands the concept of individual rights and that our government was never meant to be the massive bureaucracy it has become. We realize and understand that the Constitution of the United States gives all responsibilities not specifically designated to the federal government to the states, so that the majority of governing solutions will be enacted locally, thereby truly allowing people to govern themselves. We need to shrink the federal government. With the exception of providing our national defense, it has become one massive handout program and a mismanaged one at that. Our system has evolved into an arrangement where we send our tax dollars to Washington and then if the states operate in accordance with how the federal government wants them to, Washington will turn right around and send our money back to us under the guise of federal aid. It's truly absurd.

As we discuss further in the chapter *No Glove Fits Perfectly*, as party platforms change with the rise and fall of different leadership within the party, there will be some Republican positions that deviate from the core beliefs and do not pass the *true* conservative test. This does not negate the entire philosophy or the entire Republican Party. Regardless of whether you are a liberal or a conservative, it is doubtful that you will believe in every single position advocated by the national party platform. You are not going to agree with either viewpoint 100%.

There are currently planks in our Republican Party platform that express how we would *like* to see things done. These are our preferences and we are fairly united in these preferences. Unfortunately, this has been viewed by many as our party not being tolerant of other's beliefs or individual rights. These people may be right to some degree, and we may need to change or clarify our beliefs and positions on some issues.

This is why it's so important to learn and understand the true tenants of conservative and liberal political philosophies. It's so you will have a clear perspective and a point of view, in order to compare and determine which philosophy for the most part agrees with your core beliefs. You can't crash and burn an entire political perspective because there may be one or two positions currently supported that you don't agree with. If you take the time to learn and understand the core beliefs and actions of each party, your choice of a political philosophy should be a clear one.

CHAPTER 3

THE HISTORY AND EVOLUTION OF THE PARTIES

"If you don't know history, then you don't know anything. You are a leaf that doesn't know it is part of a tree"
- Michael Crichton

The modern day Democratic Party was founded in 1828, with its historical roots dating back to 1792, not long after our great republic was created. In the early 1790's our forefathers Thomas Jefferson and James Madison organized groups that had left the Federalist Party in part because of the fiscal policies of Alexander Hamilton.

The newly created party was named the Democratic-Republican Party and it first reached prominence in the election of 1800. The party platform consisted of a strong commitment to states' rights and to the fact that any powers and responsibilities that our Constitution did not specifically assign to the federal government would be retained by individual states.

By the 1820's the Democratic-Republican Party was the party of dominance with the Federalist

Party dwindling and basically dissolving by the late 1820's. Democratic-Republican members not happy with the party's choice of who would be the successor to President James Monroe once again spun off to form simply the Democratic Party.

Members of this new Democratic Party supported the original Jeffersonian principles set forth and a strict adherence to our Constitution. Led by Andrew Jackson, the party gained popularity quickly and along with the Whig Party were considered one of the major political parties of the day up until the 1850's when issues leading up to the Civil War emerged.

The Whig Party, which consisted of among others, wealthy business and land owners, were seen as a more commercial party representing the business interests of the day. Lacking a more broad based appeal and because of a deep divide concerning the issue of slavery, they too fell by the wayside.

Northerners had always, if not condoned, certainly looked the other way concerning the practice of slavery, but less and less had personal experience with it. The steam engines and factories of the North were leaving the South behind as still a truly agrarian (agricultural) society.

The South, with its economy dependent on producing its goods on the large plantations and getting those goods to market or to seaport for export, relied on slave labor for their economic viability.

Slaves had been escaping to the North and settling in areas where the practice of slavery was becoming all too abhorrent. Individual northern states had passed legislation regarding an escaped slave who had settled within its borders to be a free man. The Supreme Court of the United States rendered a decision stating that a resident of the northern states had no particular obligation to return an escaped slave to an owner or offer "aid and assistance" in the recovery. At the same time, President Millard Fillmore (Whig) was threatening to use the National Guard in some states to enforce previously enacted slave recovery legislation.

The country was becoming more and more divided on the issue of slavery. As a result of the Mexican-American War, the issue of how slavery would be dealt with in our newly acquired states and territories needed to be addressed...would slavery be allowed in the West? These issues were causing a great strain on our union and talk had already begun of a possible secession by the southern states. At this time our country was not even one hundred years old, the possibility of part of it splitting off to form its own country was not far-fetched.

The Compromise of 1850 was signed into law by President Millard Fillmore. Included in this compromise was the Fugitive Slave Law, an appeasement between the North and the South who had become divided geographically on the issue of slavery. This new law required that any federal marshal or other official would be subject to a $1,000 fine if they refused to arrest anyone who was alleged to be a runaway slave. Furthermore, anyone who offered aid, comfort, or shelter to an alleged runaway slave would also be subject to a $1,000 fine.

The slavery issue divided more than our country geographically. It basically ended the existence of the Whig Party, and anti-slavery members of the Democratic Party had nowhere to go. So once again, the strict constitutionalist and strong believers in personal freedom and liberty set out to start yet another political party. On March 20, 1854, founded by anti-slavery activists, the modern day Republican Party was born.

In the election of 1860, the Democratic Party was split along North and South boundaries and ended up nominating two candidates for President, effectively splitting the vote of the party. The Republican nominee, Abraham Lincoln, was the benefactor of this and was elected the 16th President of the United States.

The American Civil War and the assassination of President Lincoln should be among the most prevalent and important topics taught to our children in schools today. So fascinating are the nuances of the events leading up to the conflict; the almost unbelievable idea of our country splitting apart, the stories of deliberative military planning and strategies on both sides, and an incredible murder of a U.S. President make this subject matter one that many pursue, study, re-enact and continue to question well into their later years. The subject matter is so complex, we will not be able to go into the great detail of these events in this text.

The post war time of our country was known as Reconstruction. It was time to reunite the union and rebuild the damage done from the four years of war. Unfortunately, deep seeded resentment between the geographic regions would continue for some time to come. In the South, the Republican Party was seen as the party of the North; they had freed the slaves, and its army had burned a trail of destruction from Atlanta to the sea in Savannah. Even more than this, the Republicans, being northerners, were comprised of business owners and bankers, whose business interests created great wealth; while the South was left to rebuild itself with the remnants of its agriculture based society. Only now without the slave labor they had previously relied upon.

For these reasons white southerners despised Republicans and the Republican Party. In droves they united and joined the still intact Democratic Party. One of the party's uniting themes was that of white supremacy. The South was the solidly united Democratic stronghold. Somewhere along these times the phrase "yellow dog Democrat" was coined, referring to that in the South if the election were between a Republican and a yellow dog, the yellow dog would win every time.

Over the next fifty years, the Democratic Party remained the opposing party to the Republicans who won all but two of the Presidential elections during this time. In 1928 Herbert Hoover (R) was elected as President and had the misfortune to be in office during the Stock Market Crash of 1929. This event collapsed our currency, put most of the banks out of business; consequently millions of Americans lost their jobs. It wasn't so much that President Hoover had caused the stock market crash, as that he had presided over it. The actions he took to stabilize the economy did not work. Unlike today, there were no reserve regulations in place for lending institutions and no stop-gap trading plan for the stock exchanges. These safety measures had yet to evolve, primarily because no one ever thought this could happen. The stock market's collapse and the failures of many of the nation's financial institutions resulted in the Great Depression that lasted ten long years and is the reason for the great policy debates of today on how to properly apply regulations on business without stifling economic growth.

The Great Depression was such an impactful event on this generation and the generations to follow that in 1932, President Franklin D. Roosevelt (D) was elected to the first of his four terms and the Democrats controlled the House of Representatives almost uninterrupted from 1931 until 1995. (The 22nd Amendment was subsequently passed disallowing a President from holding office more than two terms).

The dire situation our country found herself in required swift and decisive action to address the nation's problems. Social welfare was established as a safety net so that people who were broke and had no prospect of finding a job for the foreseeable future would not starve to death. Up until this time, factory workers had to deal with poor and unsafe working conditions and there were no minimum age limits as to how old you had to be in order to work in these positions. As a result, child labor laws were passed and labor unions were established to promote safer working environments and to give the factory workers a voice against the much larger business organizations. Regulations were established and put into place for the financial regulation of banks and Wall Street as well as almost every other industry in business at the time. Roosevelt unveiled this legislation known as "The New Deal."

This initiative with the social programs, restrictive regulations, and taxes on business, as well as the establishment of labor unions was referred to as *liberal*. The opposing view point championed long-term sustained growth, low taxes, and pro-business became known as *conservative*.

In reality, there was very little else that President Roosevelt could have done in an attempt to spur the economy and re-establish the country's growth. These welfare assistance programs were necessary at the time. (However, they become a huge problem in subsequent generations when this magnitude of government intervention and redistribution was no longer required.) The New Deal which aided millions and millions of Americans and made this period more bearable for them, never really succeeded in turning the economy around. The economic data shows that even as late as 1938 the economy had been stabilized but not rebounded. That is, until the pre-war spending ramp up and subsequent World War II; that truly put this country back to work and set us up for the prosperity that would come in the post war 1950's.

During this period, black Americans who historically had voted Republican now started to align themselves with the Democratic Party. The more social welfare programs that were passed, the more the party grew. Labor union members became Democrats and with subsidies to southern and rural farmers they too joined the party. The party that post-Civil War had been popular primarily in the South was now also popular in the Northeast.

During this time, being a Republican almost became a dirty word, but the party continued to define its platform and assert its commitment to less government, lower taxes, as well as more personal freedom and responsibility. President Franklin Roosevelt died in office. Vice-President Harry S. Truman served out Roosevelt's fourth term, ran for re-election and won in 1948.

By the end of Truman's term, the country had tired of one party rule for so many years and was ready for a change. The Republicans nominated General Dwight D. Eisenhower, the victorious allied commander who oversaw operation D-Day in 1944. President Eisenhower and his Vice-President Richard M. Nixon were elected in 1952 and then again in 1956.

As is so often the case; after two successive terms of one party rule, the country swings the other way. This occurred in 1960 with the election of our first Catholic president, Democrat John F. Kennedy.

President Kennedy was assassinated on November 22, 1963 and his Vice-President Lyndon B. Johnson was sworn in. Johnson won re-election in 1964.

After this eight year Democratic run, again the country was in the mood for a change of direction. Richard M. Nixon (R) was elected in 1968 and again in 1972. President Nixon had to resign his office over the Watergate scandal and was succeeded by his Vice-President Gerald R. Ford.

President Ford has the distinction of being the first U.S. Vice-President and President that was not elected by the people's vote. Mr. Ford assumed office during a period of not only political turmoil, but also a very difficult economic time. As a result, change occurred again in 1976 with the election of President Jimmy Carter (D).

Our country's economic circumstances worsened even further under Mr. Carter and in 1980, President Ronald Reagan (R) was elected the 40th President of the United States of America. Mr. Reagan would not use this phrase until his re-election campaign of 1984, but it was now "Morning Again in America."

President Reagan served for two terms and was succeeded by his Vice-President George H.W. Bush (R). President Bush served only one term and was succeeded by President William Jefferson (Bill) Clinton (D). President Clinton served two terms and was succeeded by President George W. Bush (R) who also served two terms. In 2008, the United States elected its first black president, Barack Obama (D).

So looking back, from 1920-2012 we have elected Democrats and Republicans to serve an equal number of terms. Twelve terms for Democrats and twelve terms for Republicans. It's hard to ignore the almost complete pattern of two terms of one party, followed by two terms of the other.

WHY YOUR FATHER'S A REPUBLICAN

CHAPTER FOUR

THINGS LIBERALS WILL NEVER UNDERSTAND

"There is nothing more dangerous, than sincere ignorance"
- Dr. Martin Luther King, Jr.

There is No Utopia

Webster's defines the word utopia as "a place of ideal perfection especially in laws, government, and social conditions."

Wikipedia defines the word as "an imagined place or state of things in which everything is perfect."

Liberals often have a utopian view of the world. They view it how they think it should be and take measures to make it that way. Conservatives view the world how it is and try to make it better.

Liberals tend to think with their hearts... Conservatives tend to think with their heads.

It has been said that a conservative strives for an equal opportunity for all, while a liberal strives for an equal outcome.

The bottom line is THERE IS NO UTOPIA! Things will never be the way you want them to be, just because you want them to. To say nothing of the fact that everyone has different opinions of how things should be. We don't operate in a vacuum, outside forces will always exist. We simply cannot control the minds and actions of other people.

Instead of working toward making the world the ideal utopia you think it should be, I hope you will take the time to educate yourself and observe the world as it truly is, then work to make it a better place.

The Folly of Gun Control

The biggest misconception liberals have about gun control laws is that criminals will obey them. Criminals, by definition do not obey the law. They don't obey the laws against theft, rape, or murder, yet the lynch pin of the liberal argument for more gun control laws is that by disarming private citizens we will all be safer. The reality is, of course, that only the law-abiding citizens will be disarmed and will be completely defenseless against those who wish to do them harm or steal their property.

The premise behind many liberal beliefs is the utopian concept that people will do what you ask them to do, simply because you ask them to do it.

The truth is, the crime rate is higher in areas where the expectation of being met with an armed resistance is least expected. For example, how many shootings do you hear about at a gun store or a police station where possessing a firearm is to be expected verses known gun free zones like schools or college campuses?

The cities and municipalities that have strict gun laws, meaning their laws are more restrictive on law-abiding citizens, have a documented higher crime rate than those cities that recognize our Second Amendment right to protect ourselves. The higher crime rate clearly correlates to the fact that non-law-abiding citizens know that they will not be met with an armed resistance if they wish to assault someone.

The liberal answer to how we end the large number of murders committed with firearms occurring each year in the United States is ultimately to pass laws curtailing the rights of private citizens to own or possess a firearm. They cannot start out with an all-inclusive argument. As with most liberal reforms, they recognize that gradual shifts will be required to reach their ultimate goal. This is referred to as a "slippery slope." Once you begin going down it, there is no telling how far you will go. First, it will be weapons that look scary. Then they will take advantage of every unfortunate act of violence reported in the media that occurs using a firearm.

The horrific school shooting that occurred in Newtown, Connecticut is one of the worst crimes a person can hear of, especially for a parent of school-aged children. This event, while absolutely horrendous is being used by the left to argue for the banning of AR-15 assault-style weapons in the civilian marketplace. This act was committed by a mentally deranged individual who obtained his weapons by stealing them. If he had not stolen an AR-15, he would have stolen and used another type of firearm. The result would have been the same.

It's not the inanimate firearm that perpetrates violence; violence is the result of an individual's actions. Many on the left are using this heart-wrenching event as a reason to enact a federal assault weapons ban. This is not the answer. In 1999, there was another mass school shooting at Columbine High School using an assault weapon. An assault weapons ban had been passed by Congress five years earlier. The shooters in this occurrence were also in possession of the firearms illegally.

The pertinent common thread in all of the mass shootings we hear of is not that the gunmen were all in possession of a firearm, but that they all suffered from some degree of mental illness. This is the issue to be addressed - not to violate a free people's right to bear arms. Do we need a reasonable system to perform criminal background checks as well as a safeguard against a mentally unstable individual gaining access to a firearm? Of course we do.

In May 2013, the U.S. Department of Justice issued a special report, *Firearm Violence, 1993-2011*. The stated highlights of the report include: "*Firearm-related homicides declined 39% from 1993 to 2011, Non-fatal firearm crimes declined 69% from 1993 to 2011, 70%-80% of firearm homicides and 90% of non-fatal firearm victimizations were committed with a handgun from 1993-2011, in 2004, among state prison inmates who possessed a gun at the time of the offense, less than 2% bought their firearm at a flea market or gun show and 40% obtained their firearm from and illegal source.*"

There are approximately 50 million more guns in America now than in 1993. This report directly refutes the long held liberal belief that more guns equal more crime. It is almost unbelievable that this report was issued by Attorney General Eric Holder's Justice Department, as Mr. Holder is a

Democratic Presidential appointee.

This is yet another example of how when examining an issue liberals stop at the first and most simplistic answer they come across. People are getting killed with guns = let's get rid of all the guns. More guns = more gun violence. No, actually gun violence is perpetrated for the most part by individuals who are breaking the law. By increasing gun ownership among law-abiding citizens you are providing a deterrent to this violence. Therefore, you cannot make the simplistic argument that more guns = more gun violence. This is now confirmed by a real world experiment and the data has been confirmed by the U.S. Justice Department.

Regarding the liberal quest to remove firearms from the hands of law-abiding citizens, we are not speaking of rifles and shotguns used for hunting and sport, liberals insist they will make allowances for these. Primarily, we are speaking of handguns because statistics do show that hand- guns are used to commit the majority of violent acts that occur with a firearm. Handguns are also the most common firearm used for personal protection by law-abiding citizens.

It is important to note that the Second Amendment to the Constitution of the United States does not simply allow for "long guns" to be used for hunting or sport. Actually, the Second Amendment does not address *hunting* in any way, shape or form. When liberals inject hunting into this conversation, it is merely a *red herring*; a specious argument so that they may knock it down by saying "You don't need that kind of weapon to hunt" or "Don't worry, we're okay with hunting."

The Second Amendment provides for the right, and some would say, the responsibility for private citizens to be able to maintain a "militia" in order to combat tyranny from a government that possesses weapons, and the legal authority to use them. Inherent in this right, is the right to protect one's self, our family, and our property from harm.

You will undoubtedly be asked over and over by your liberal friends "why do we need weapons like an AR-15 to be legal?" The answer to why a law-abiding citizen needs to have access to semi-automatic weapons is quite simply because non-law-abiding citizens have access to them.

Starting in the late 1970's the United States began a major campaign called the "War on Drugs" which still continues today. Our government committed itself to the enforcement of our drug laws, particularly regarding the importation of drugs entering our country from Mexico.

Preventing illegal drugs from entering into our

country was declared to be among our nation's top priorities. A tremendous amount of resources (billions of dollars) have been spent trying to keep illegal drugs out of our country. Yet today after almost forty years of this, you can still buy illegal drugs on the street corner of any major city in America. When our government tries to tell you they can ban certain weapons, keeping them out of the hands of criminals, thereby eliminating your need to own one for your own defense, don't believe it.

One final example: In June 2013 in Santa Monica, California a lone gunman murdered four people and injured five others while reportedly carrying an AR-15 style "assault" rifle. In California, assault weapons are illegal, 30 round magazines are illegal, as is concealing a weapon without a permit. All of these laws were broken on that day. Since the gunman escaped into the "gun free zone" of a college campus he was met with zero resistance until law enforcement could arrive and with *their* firearms ended the threat.

Compare the college campus "gun free zone" to the streets of our communities if gun control advocates had their way. It is often repeated that "when seconds count, the police are minutes away."

We have to be careful to avoid the slippery slope

but there is little reason to not strengthen the criminal background checks that are presently required when purchasing a firearm. Background checks to stop criminals, not law-abiding citizens. These background checks should also include some method of being able to distinguish which individuals are not mentally competent to own a weapon. This will not be an easy task as a person's medical records are private and currently no such database exists. Still as the number of armed assaults by mentally deranged people continues to increase, something must be done to keep firearms out of their hands, without restricting the rights of law-abiding citizens.

If liberals had their way, we would severely curtail the private ownership of handguns and semi-automatic weapons and all of the law-abiding citizens would turn their guns in. The non-law-abiding citizens would not. Of course these are the same people who are committing rapes, robberies, and murders, and now they will know that their victims have been disarmed. Our Constitution gives us the right to life, liberty, and the pursuit of happiness. It also gives us the tools in order to maintain these rights.

How Social Programs Have Negatively Affected the Poor

There may be no better example to illustrate how the misguided utopian concept of liberalism leads to unintended consequences than to evaluate the effect of social welfare programs over the past forty years. In the mid-1960's liberals tried to "out liberal" each other. President Johnson, after signing the Civil Rights Act of 1964 and Voting Rights Act of 1965 sought to expand upon his newfound popularity with blacks and to rebuild relationships with rural southern whites. A war on poverty was declared and Johnson proposed and later enacted his "Great Society" legislation. Senator Robert F. Kennedy was going to be Johnson's primary competition for the Democratic nomination in 1968 and began an early campaign which included among other things photo opportunity trips to rural Appalachia and the Deep South showcasing and documenting the plight of these poverty-stricken people.

The need to help these people was undeniable but as usual the enactment of permanent legislation which offered a hand out, rather than temporary help, and a hand up, created what is known today as "generational welfare." During the first generation, this aid was needed and undoubtedly increased the quality of life for those who received it.

Beginning in the second generation, it became easier for some recipients to see that they didn't have to try and find work to feed their families. The government would pay them welfare to cover the cost of their living expenses. There is a correlation to be found between these programs and the Bible quote "give a man a fish and feed him for the day, teach a man to fish and feed him for a lifetime."

By the third generation, many of these people had no desire to find a job to support and feed their family. They even came to realize that government welfare provided them more money than if they went out and got a job. At this point, they were receiving welfare for living expenses, food stamps for food, housing vouchers for rent, and medical care from the Medicaid system. These entitlement programs were set up to provide assistance based on family size. This created an explosion of welfare babies: if a mother increased her number of children, she knew that not only would she not be responsible for any of the medical costs associated with giving birth to these children, but her monthly checks for welfare and other assistance would increase. To further poison the well, the social program administrators (who were just *trying* to help), operated the program in a way that if there was not an adult male (a father figure) in the household, the mother's assistance would be greater than if there were. Can you guess what family structure this led to?

Entitlements used to refer to programs that people had paid into and would expect to receive a benefit from, they would be entitled to it. If the government required you to have money withheld from your paycheck in order to contribute to the Social Security program, you would then be entitled to receive Social Security benefits when you become eligible for the program. If the government offered you a guaranteed medical benefit for the rest of your life as an incentive to join our military forces, then after you were discharged you would be entitled to this benefit. This is what used to be known as an entitlement; you contributed to the program in order to receive a benefit. Today however, apparently to make it harder to debate this topic, welfare benefits such as Section 8 Housing, food stamps, the WIC (Women, Infants, and Children) program, and many other forms of government support are now lumped in with, and referred to as, entitlements, even though these people have not contributed to these programs. These programs are paid for by our tax dollars. Could referring to these programs as entitlements be the reason why so many Americans feel they are *entitled* to receive free housing, free food, and a free check for the other expenses they incur in life? Could this be why so many today feel that they are not responsible for taking care of themselves and that the government is?

So here we are almost fifty years after the enactment of these programs with unwed mothers as young as sixteen years old being provided with their own apartments, not allowing the fathers of the babies to stick around, certainly not getting married, receiving free housing, food stamps, welfare, and medical care. When they decide they need an increase in income, they already know they simply need to have another baby.

An unwed mother with four children receives enough government assistance to equal the compensation of someone who gets out of bed every day, goes to work, and earns thirty-five thousand dollars per year.

Who would you expect these people to vote for? The party that wishes to reform these programs and re-instill hope and self-respect, or the party that simply promises more and more of the same? Plus you don't have to go rob somebody to get your money; the government will do that for you and send you a check, direct deposit in your account, or put it on your EBT card.

This "generational welfare" also explains why we have natural born citizens in this country that have lived here for decades claiming that they just can't make it because of being held down by "the man" or because of "racism" or whatever excuse they want to use. At the same time, we have immigrants who come to this country not even knowing how to speak the language, not knowing anyone, and many times *truly* being discriminated against. Through hard work, perseverance, and a no-excuse attitude, they are most often successful if not the first generation, then certainly by the second one.

Freedom Does Not Guarantee Us Success, Just Opportunity

There is a fallacy in liberal dogma that since some people in life are successful, while others are not, this clearly demonstrates our system is inherently unfair and justifies the right to be able to take (confiscate) from the rich to give (redistribute) to the poor.

This belief totally ignores the actions and initiative taken by the successful person and how generally speaking, all of us are different. We all have different motivators and desires in life. Furthermore, being successful in any endeavor is primarily a function of two factors. Making logical decisions and putting forth enough effort to achieve the goal or task.

At school, when everyone in class is given an assignment, does everyone receive the same grade? Of course not. Some people will exert more effort than others, some will care what grade they receive, some will not. If it is your objective to get a good grade, you will do what needs to be done in order to be successful. If you don't take your assignment seriously and are not willing to invest the appropriate time and effort, you will most likely not be successful. This is the same as it is in real life, grown-up life, if you will.

If you let yourself be distracted, make poor choices, or take the path of immediate gratification, you are probably not going to be successful. On the other hand, if you make sound decisions, pay attention, and postpone gratification in return for attaining a longer term goal, you *will* typically be rewarded.

What would it be like to attend a school where all of the A students were required to give up that grade and take a B so that the D students could have their grade raised to a C ? Could you imagine any circumstances that would make this scenario fair?

This example is not unlike the philosophical division in our society; why some people vote Democrat and some Republican. If you were an A student you wouldn't be in favor of this plan at all. If you were a D student you would be all for it. If you were an A student that felt sorry for the D students, you might consider it. In a lot of ways this illustrates the liberal verses conservative debate.

Could you ever imagine a scenario where the individuals who made the right choices, stayed out of trouble, postponed immediate gratification and made personal sacrifices in order to be successful, were told they were simply more fortunate than those who did the exact opposite, and were then required to give compensation to these less fortunate?

Wouldn't it be preposterous to penalize the behavior you want and reward the behavior you don't?

Again, in many ways these kinds of questions are what the debate about being a liberal, or being a conservative, is all about.

Since we are speaking of school, let's talk about public school in America. The cost to attend is free, take of advantage of it or don't, it's your choice, but don't pop up later in life and claim you did not have access to the same opportunities.

While going through life you will be confronted with different choices and opportunities. Use wisely your power of choice and remember that as Americans we are not guaranteed the outcome of success. We are guaranteed the right to an equal opportunity.

Liberals vs. Evil Corporations

Liberals love to bash evil corporations. Corporations are the big, bad companies that oppress the working class, take unfair advantage of their workers while retaining huge profits for themselves and then ultimately move their operations overseas to dodge paying U.S. income taxes.

Now for the reality... a corporation is a legal business entity, made up of shareholders and governed by a board of directors. Do you know who the owners of America's mega corporations are? They are your parents, your aunts and uncles, your grandparents, and ironically your (liberal) teachers.

If you ask all of the aforementioned people, you will find out that some of them actually own stock in these companies. For the most part though, Americans own pieces of these corporations through their retirement accounts. Many people hold these individual stocks in their IRAs. Many more own them by virtue of an index fund that owns a piece of all the stocks listed in an index like the S&P 500. The two major institutional owners of these stocks are large insurance companies and teacher retirement funds.

The corporate income tax in the U.S. is among the

highest in the industrialized world at up to 35%. There is a strong case to be made that corporations don't actually pay income tax, since these taxes, as business expenses, are used in the computation to establish profit margins for goods and services and ultimately are passed on to the consumer. Therefore, when liberals push for an increase in the income tax rates on corporations, they are really just increasing the cost of goods. The end consumer will ultimately end up paying for it via higher prices. In other words, Democrats end up hurting the people they claim they are trying to help.

Putting that line of thinking aside for a moment consider this, U.S. corporations pay 35% in corporate income tax on the income they generate. They then turn around and pay out these profits to stockholders in the form of interest, dividends, and capital gains. The individual stockholder must then report this as income and once again pay income tax on these same profits. This amounts to double taxation. The income tax is first paid by the corporation, then again by the individual. So not only is our corporate tax rate among the highest in the world, these profits are taxed twice.

U.S. corporations don't want to move their operations overseas. They are forced to by increasing government regulations and increased labor costs in our country. Outsourcing labor and off-shoring some operations however does not exempt these companies from paying U.S. income taxes. The only way a corporation can do this is by relocating their headquarters to a foreign land. Some have decided that our tax and regulatory burden is too oppressive and have done this, but most thankfully have not.

Either way, we have liberals insisting that more government controls and regulations be placed onto corporate America. Then, if successful in achieving this, they ridicule big business for wanting to move their operations to more business-friendly environments. Liberals do not understand business.

Please consider these facts when a liberal is bemoaning evil corporations; don't let them talk about your relatives and your teachers like that.

Third World Famine and Hunger - What Doesn't Work

In 1969, I entered the first grade. At Halloween, the public school I attended gave each student a little box with a coin slot in it and told us we should (while trick-or-treating) solicit and collect money for The United Nations Children's Fund (UNICEF.) After Halloween, the school would collect all of the donations and send them to this organization so that we could end the starvation in

Africa. Like the good little ambassadors that we were, this is exactly what we did, that year and for several years thereafter.

It was not uncommon to see pictures on the evening news of children starving in Africa. The pooched-out bellies (from starvation) and the swarming flies made it easy to want to help, not only feed these children now, but also help to end the massive famine that was said to be the root cause of this tragedy. If we would help now, this atrocity could end.

Fast forward forty-plus years and I happen to see this same solicitation brought home at Halloween by my son. Hmmm, seems the call for help is just as urgent, how could this be? Certainly this organization has received billions in aid over the past half century, not to mention the billions sent in relief efforts by the United States and other countries. How could this be??

Now, obviously, helping the less fortunate and those that are in need is a truly noble cause. I believe that everyone who has the means should give back to society, by whatever means they choose. At what point does someone examine an effort to remedy a problem that has grown increasingly worse over the past fifty years?

In search of answers, I went to the organization's

website. Right off the bat it tells me that every day over 19,000 children die that don't have to. The pleas for donations are just as heart-wrenching as they were in 1969 when this fifty year old was in the first grade. Whatever UNICEF is doing, it's obviously not working.

I was happy to see that at some point along the way, there was a spin-off of sorts. There is now a separate UN fund called the United States Fund. The United Nations is one of the most corrupt organizations in the world. When the word corrupt doesn't apply, the word inept does. Billions of dollars in aid have been wasted by the UN letting food and other resources rot while internally arguing about how best to distribute them, or by delivering aid to tribal rulers and dictators who stood in the way of these resources getting to the masses. So it was nice to see that a separate spin-off fund had been established specifically for the contributions of the United States.

The site lists all of the worthy endeavors this organization attempts to fulfill, from emergency relief, clean water and sanitation, to providing food and medicine. Again, all noble causes but this appears to be a classic example and proof positive, that the liberal philosophy of simply throwing money at a problem and hoping it will go away, is not the answer.

How President Reagan Won the Cold War

If you were a child of the 1950's you would have to perform air raid drills and crawl under your school desk while an air raid siren blared. The Soviet threat was real.

The Soviet Union was our mortal enemy and we faced off against them time and time again in North Korea, Cuba, and Vietnam. It was truly the "Cold War" with secret spy espionage taking place on both sides in order to procure information about what the other was doing.

In what is known as the "nuclear arms race" both sides possessed enough nuclear weapons to destroy the other many times over. In an effort to demonstrate who had the superior defense capabilities, it truly came down to a race to see how many missiles and warheads we could amass and point at the other to ensure the other country would never attempt an offensive strike. This is how we lived from the 1950's into the 60's, 70's and finally the 1980's.

By the time President Ronald Reagan was elected in 1980, it had already become apparent that communism was not working in the Soviet Union. Americans saw pictures of community grocery stores (where Soviets would go for their weekly supply of government provided food) with almost bare shelves. Reports of severe rationing were commonplace in our news.

It was also apparent that the Russians had been pumping tremendous amounts of resources into their defense programs to keep up with the United States in the arms race... resources that were diverted from being used for the welfare of the people.

President Reagan introduced very firm policies toward Russia and made it clear we were capable of maintaining and enforcing our positions. Through his diplomatic summits with Russian President Mikhail Gorbachev, Mr. Reagan represented our strength while maintaining a warm and personable relationship with Mr. Gorbachev.

Liberals often cite President Reagan's defense spending as a reason our country ran a federal deficit of over one trillion dollars for the first time in history. They also ridiculed his missile defense program SDI (Strategic Defense Initiative) which was dubbed "Star Wars" because it was so technologically advanced and seemed to be something right out of the science fiction books and movies.

The only way President Reagan could get the Democratic Congress to maintain our defense budget was to compromise and allow their massive spending on social programs. These spending programs are what actually created the trillion dollar deficits, but it was necessary to do so. The fact that Mr. Reagan also presided over the economic plan that began our country's greatest period of peace-time prosperity more than made up for these deficits. Even though the dollar amount of the federal deficit grew, thanks to Reagan's economic expansion, the deficit, as a percentage of our nation's GDP, actually went down. This means our productivity went up while our debt went down.

The truth of the matter is that President Ronald Reagan ended the cold war with the Russians without firing a shot. Yes, the defense budget skyrocketed, but what price can you put on being safe from the nuclear threat that our country lived with for forty years? The kind of threat that had school children performing practice drills under their desks at school and had Americans building bomb shelters and storing rations in their basement in case of a nuclear event. The answer, of course, is that you cannot place a price on the removal of this threat. This victory was priceless.

After the Soviet Union fell, top level Russian diplomats conceded that with resources already stretched to the point of starving their own people, trying to keep up with the U.S.'s "Star Wars" defense system was an unfathomable situation.

George W. Bush Did Not Steal the 2000 Election

Once again, I lived through this; I saw the events as they unfolded firsthand. The 2000 presidential election was between Democratic nominee, the current Vice-President Al Gore and the Republican nominee, former Texas Governor and son of our 41st President, George W. Bush. Election nights for me are like the Super Bowl and this one went on for a while. Flipping between channels to see who was reporting what...absolutely exhilarating!

To this day, there are still Democrats that believe George W. Bush was handed the presidential election by virtue of a decision by the U.S. Supreme Court to end an illegal recount that was being conducted in a few counties in the state of Florida.

At the time, just about every Democrat believed George W. Bush stole the Presidency after the election results were reported. I worked with some folks who were members of various minority groups and diehard liberals, and they honestly believed there was a conspiracy perpetrated by the highest levels of the United States government to alter the results of the presidential election.

Let's start near the beginning of the evening. Polls in the Eastern Time zone of the United States closed at 7:00 p.m. At that time, NBC News reported that they were projecting that Al Gore had won the vote in the state of Florida.

News outlets were not supposed to make projections until a state's election polling places had closed, because it could influence the turnout. People who had not yet voted, when hearing their candidate had already lost, would most likely not follow-through and cast their vote.

The problem with NBC's 7:00 p.m. EST projection was that the Florida panhandle area is on Central Time, an hour behind, so their polls were still open for another hour. The Panhandle is historically known to be a Republican stronghold with many conservatives and active-duty military living there. We'll come back to this in a minute.

The election results were very close all night, 270 electoral votes were needed to win. After much nail-biting and several network projections having to be reversed, it was all coming down to the state of Florida and their 25 electoral votes. Networks that had earlier projected that Gore would win Florida were now projecting that Bush had won, but all of the votes had not yet been counted, and some of these counties were heavy Democratic strongholds. Later and later it went on. I watched news icon David Brinkley mistakenly utter something he shouldn't have at about 2:00 a.m. because he didn't realize they were back from the commercial break. It was no big deal, but I had to grimace when he so nonchalantly said "We're not on the air" only to be rebuked by Sam Donaldson saying "Oh, yes we are!"

Vice-President Gore actually called candidate Bush to offer his congratulations and concede defeat...only to later call back and withdraw his remarks.

On and on it went and we would not know the outcome of the election for more than a month because of endless recounts of various counties within Florida.

What occurred in Florida during that period was mind boggling. Mr. Gore had requested a hand counting of ballots in just four counties, counties that were heavily Democratic. The Florida Supreme Court weighed in and ordered the recount of additional ballots that had not been machine counted because the machine could not make out which hole had been punched out, or if it had been punched out completely. Our nation became familiar with the term "hanging chad" that referred to that little piece of paper that gets punched out of a Scantron form, like you use in your standardized tests. The news reports were that Bush was ahead by only 300 hundred votes, then ahead by 900 votes, on and on. Different counties began to apply different procedures for conducting recounts. Not surprisingly, some methods appeared to be biased toward favoring one candidate or the other, it was a bit weird and a disconcerting time to live through. In the end, the Supreme Court of the United States, in a 5-4 decision put an end to all recounts and ordered the state officials to certify the election results that were indicating that George W. Bush would be our 43rd President.

The liberal media airwaves were lit up reporting that President-Elect George W. Bush had stolen the election. The mainstream media took it upon themselves to begin conducting recounts. In the meantime, President Bush was sworn into office.

The first recounts were conducted by the *Miami Herald* and *USA Today*. The results showed that under most generally accepted criteria that George W. Bush won the election. Finally, a study commissioned by eight of the country's most influential newspapers concluded that George W. Bush did indeed win the Florida vote.

Since this time, a number of revised assessments have been made that assert these findings were false, but this is just partisan politics.

By the way, a comparison was made of the Florida panhandle voting results. The votes cast for Republicans in year 2000 were noticeably off from previous years. The most likely explanation was the erroneous media reporting of the projection that Al Gore had already won the state before all of the polls had actually closed. If adjusted to be proportional to previous year's elections, Mr. Bush would have received thousands of additional votes.

There Was WMD!

So often in the media we hear that President George W. Bush was wrong about there being Weapons of Mass Destruction (WMD) in Iraq; therefore our entire reasoning for invading that country in 2003 was bogus and unfounded. This statement has been repeated so many times, the vast majority of Americans undoubtedly believe it.

I watched the events leading up to the Iraqi invasion occur. I watched the reporting of these events every night from multiple news sources. After the invasion and occupation, I could never understand why members of the Republican Party could not effectively refute the erroneous assertions that were made about the existence of WMD in Iraq.

What I saw reported was that we had satellite photographs of truck caravans from known Iraqi military sites in a mass exodus from that country heading into Syria. UN inspectors found missiles and chemical war heads that the Iraqi government said had been previously destroyed. Iraq repeatedly fired on allied forces reconnaissance aircraft and jets that were enforcing the Northern No-Fly Zone. Iraqi President Saddam Hussein refused to allow his scientists and their families to leave the country or to be interviewed by UN inspectors.

We knew Hussein had WMD because he had previously used them against his own people, the Kurds, in 1991. Furthermore, the United Nations Security Council issued an order (#1441) for Hussein to allow UN inspectors in to confirm that these WMD had been destroyed and if they could not provide such evidence, UN member nations had authorization to use "all means necessary" to make Iraq comply with this order. Hussein would not allow unfettered access and eventually the UN inspectors left the country.

The U.S. invaded Iraq in compliance with the UN Security Council order, in which 22 countries agreed that evidence of WMD existed and that Hussein must allow for inspections or be compelled to comply. It had long been rumored that France and Russia had supplied Iraq with conventional-style weapons, thus violating the embargo sanctions in place by the UN. When a vote was taken to compel Iraq to comply with the Security Council order or face invasion, there were a few countries that sought to delay this action. Among them...France and Russia.

After the invasion of Iraq, a number of high level scientists were given asylum in foreign countries and confirmed they had been working on chemical and WMD projects.

It just doesn't make sense. If Saddam Hussein *did* comply with United Nations Security Council order #1441 and destroyed all of his existing and future WMD capabilities, why would he not allow the UN inspectors to confirm this, instead of losing billions of dollars in oil revenue as a result of sanctions and ultimately losing his country and his life?

In 2005, the CIA released a report stating that we never found WMD in Iraq.

It is a true statement that we never *found* WMD in Iraq after the invasion, but to say that we were wrong (or lied) about the existence of WMD in Iraq would be, to say the least, disingenuous.

Bill Clinton Had a Lot of Help

Bill Clinton was a Democratic Party President that receives a lot of credit (from Democrats) for leading the way on certain societal change issues and re-invigorating a sputtering economy. Mr. Clinton was elected in 1992 with 43% of the popular vote. Third party candidate, businessman H. Ross Perot got just enough of the vote to prevent the re-election of President George H.W. Bush. Almost immediately, Mr. Clinton was embroiled in controversy and scandals. In the 1994 mid-term elections, after only two years, America had already had enough and elected a majority Republican Congress with the House of Representatives going Republican for the first time in sixty years.

Mr. Clinton was able to pass a tax increase in 1993 that would later be held up by some as one of the reasons our economy took off during his terms in office. If you go back and look at the GDP (growth) numbers for that period, you actually see that the economy remained fairly flat for a few years after that tax hike and did not actually take off until 1997 when the internet run-up was occurring. There had also been a Republican-led tax cut. The internet and other technological advances changed how America did business and the productivity gains were unbelievable. When the "tech bubble" burst in the year 2000, the economy once again returned to sub-par performance and most Democrats don't realize this, but President Clinton left office with two successive dismal quarters, thus leaving President George W. Bush with a recession as he entered office. Then, of course, a mere eight months after taking office, President Bush was faced with the events of 9/11 which greatly impacted our economy. Through tax and fiscal policy, President

Bush's team was able to not only keep us from being attacked again during his terms, but also guide us out of this recession. President George W. Bush does not get enough credit for these actions. Most Americans believe George W. Bush was responsible for the de-regulation that allowed Wall Street to run rampant and engage in activities that caused the economic crash in 2008. It was however, President Bill Clinton that signed the legislation providing for the de-regulation of the banking industry in the year 2000.

How Lower Tax Rates Increase Productivity and Government Revenues

For most of us, common sense tells us that if we increase the income tax rate on Americans that tax revenues to the U.S. Treasury will go up, and if we decrease these tax rates, revenues will go down. Simple addition and subtraction, right?

Wrong!

We further explore this in our chapter *A Quick Lesson on Economics* but let me review it here in a nutshell. History has shown us that during the recessions of the early 1960's and the early 1980's when tax rates were decreased that actual revenue to the U.S. Treasury in the form of income taxes actually increased.

This is because a higher income tax rate is a disincentive to those who want to work harder in order to earn more money. For example, if the government is going to take forty cents of every dollar you earn up to $50,000 per year, and fifty cents of every dollar you earn after that, many will simply say it's not worth it to spend the money on transportation, child care, and all of the other expenses associated with making more money. But if the government were to, let's say reduce the tax rate on the first $50,000 earned to twenty-five cents on every dollar, and then reduce the rate to thirty-five cents per dollar on any amount over that, many people would start working over-time or even take second jobs. They would increase their work activities in order to make and keep more money. Not only will they be keeping a larger share of what they presently earn, they will be incentivized to work harder, be more productive, and end up earning more than they did previously. They will then be paying a lower percentage rate, but a higher overall dollar amount to the government in the form of income taxes; the government collects more revenue.

Wealthier people will risk more capital to fund investments because now the reward will be greater on the profits they receive. When people's incomes rise, so does their tax liability. Even though the tax rate is lower, they are being taxed on a larger amount which helps to make up the difference. It doesn't stop there. What our economy receives in return is a boost in productivity. This creates more jobs and opportunities. All of these newly employed people are now paying income taxes where before they didn't even have a job, and were paying zero in income taxes, and were probably *taking* money from our system. Reducing the taxable burden creates more individual productivity and more disposable income to purchase goods and services which creates more jobs and will enable a sustainable path to growth and prosperity. By increasing tax rates, you penalize productivity which lowers growth and will actually decrease the amount of money collected in the form of income taxes.

Again, we will cover economics in greater detail in Chapter Six but don't fall victim to "simple" math or simple behavior assessments; we do not live in a vacuum, every action has a reaction.

Affirmative Action is Racial Discrimination

There was a time in this country when racism, bigotry, and prejudice was allowed to affect hiring decisions and thus enabled unqualified individuals to be hired over qualified individuals of a specific race. This, of course, was wrong, but to be expected for a period of time until the concept of equal rights was truly understood, accepted, and applied.

In the early 1960's, a program known as "affirmative action" was created and implemented through an executive order signed by President John F. Kennedy. The intention was to prevent discrimination against employees or applicants for employment, on the basis of "color, religion, sex, or national origin." The program first applied to the federal government and to all entities doing business with the federal government. From there, it was applied to admission policies of public colleges and universities.

This program set out to equalize the process for minorities (blacks, women, etc.) in order to make sure that the best person for the job did indeed receive it. It was conceived so that it would truly "level the playing field" for the best qualified candidates when it came to employment, college acceptance and other positions which should be truly attained based on one's individual merit and be totally unaffected by other criteria, such as their sex or race.

Along the way, the concept evolved into not only leveling the playing field but giving the minority an advantage. If two equally qualified candidates were up for promotion or admission, the one who was a member of a designated minority was required, by law to receive this position.

Then it went further, if multiple candidates were

up for a position and a lesser qualified individual of minority status was among them, affirmative action required the lesser qualified individual receive the position, because they had historically been disadvantaged. This situation was caused by either overt or covert "quota systems" that had been developed requiring that a certain number of each minority should be included in the work force.

So, the United States government with the intention of making it illegal to discriminate in these selection processes, based on an individual's race or sex, created a solution to the problem that discriminated against equally and sometimes better qualified individuals based on their sex and race. This irony has become known as "reverse discrimination."

While the intention of these policies (at the time) was good and necessary, it should have simply been enough to make it illegal to discriminate against anyone based on race, color, gender, national origin, or sexual orientation. Period, end of story. Anyone means anyone.

Again, it is a liberal utopian belief that we can right all of the wrongs that man has done to man since the beginning of time. It simply cannot be done, and is foolish to try.

It's also a utopian belief that we can rid each person's belief system when it comes to discrimination and racial bias. We cannot. Just as it is impossible to legislate morality, it is also impossible to legislate what a person thinks.

Even today, I personally have encountered individuals of one race who simply will never "like" individuals of another race. These beliefs are just a part of them, it's how they were raised, and it is how they will feel until the day they die. But that's okay. People are free to believe whatever it is they want to believe as long as their actions do not infringe upon the rights of another. As a people, once we surrender the freedom of our own thoughts, we are finished.

If I were a black person in our society today, and I was told that I would receive preferential treatment because of the color of my skin, I would be offended on the outside, but more importantly, on the inside I would always wonder, if society bestows this belief upon me, that I need this advantage, is it true, am I of lesser quality? Of course, the answer to that question is NO.

As a white person in our society today, I am often confronted with the argument that historically, black individuals may not have had the same advantages that I have had when it comes to education. In this day and time, we all have the same opportunities for education. The education system in our country is free; all you have to do is show enough initiative to attend. If some have not been able to take advantage of it, this needs to be addressed within the individual households and within the culture that permeates some segments of both black and white society.

As a society, we need to get over this stigma between black and white, it has been one hundred fifty years since anyone has owned any slaves or picked any cotton. Since the dawn of time there have been oppressors and the oppressed. Just read the Bible, no one people has an exclusive claim to having been oppressed. The sooner we all treat each other as individuals instead of as a class of people or as a member of a minority, the better off we will all be.

Labor Unions

There was a time in our country when labor unions were necessary. During our industrial revolution, issues regarding workplace safety, reasonable working hours and conditions, as well as child labor laws were very relevant. As time went on, workplace rules and regulations were made to apply to everyone, not only to certain industries like steel mills and coal mines. The safe work-place and fair wage laws applied to everyone in the country, but certain industries continued to have their labor force represented by unions. This was helpful when it came to negotiating contracts for large groups. Instead of having to deal with each individual worker, the labor groups could collectively bargain and what one got, they all got. Labor unions such as the steel workers, the auto workers, railroad and trucking workers helped build this country. There came a time however when the negotiating demands of the unions caused certain American industries to not be competitive with worldwide competition.

Simply put labor unions demand a higher wage than the free market would set for the cost of labor; this causes an increase in cost to the employer, who then in turn must raise the cost of their goods or services to the customer. If other domestic or foreign companies operate without union labor, the cost of their goods and services will be available at a cheaper cost for the consumer. At some point, this causes the union employer to be non-competitive and may even put the company out of business.

Some companies have gone out of business when they could not get their unions to accept concessions in their labor agreement. Other industries have actually disappeared from our country because market forces for the cost of labor were trumped by escalating wage and benefit packages to unions.

U.S. corporations are demonized for sending their manufacturing jobs overseas, in reality; in many cases you can thank unions for this. Worldwide economic forces dictate a competitive labor market, unfortunately labor unions do not allow for this.

Unions inflate the cost of less qualified workers and protect unproductive workers from discipline or firing.

Using the United Auto Workers as an example, it is said that union retirement benefits have gotten so out of hand, that roughly five thousand dollars of the cost of a new American-made automobile is attributable to these costs.

Labor union leaders and members vote almost exclusively Democratic. This is no surprise, as obviously, Republicans, being pro-business, pro-productivity, and pro-individual rights would like to see the influence of unions greatly decrease. This will happen naturally over time, the union model of productivity cannot sustain itself.

Democratic candidates pander to these unions because historically they have always been able to count on their votes. Even so, occasionally you will see a politician slip and forget which demographic group they are speaking to. I will never forget during the Presidential election of

1996, I was watching C-SPAN and the program "Road to the White House," C-SPAN would follow the candidates and record them as usual, unfiltered, with no commentary attempting to explain to you what you are hearing. They would follow the candidates through the week and then present a condensed version of the itinerary at the end of the week. I watched then Vice-President Al Gore campaigning somewhere in the South towing the party line. At one point, his comments focused on labor and the right to work, etc., and while I do not remember his actual words it was apparent that he was denouncing labor union practices and promoting free unfettered employment practices. Given the region of the country he was addressing this was met with great cheers of approval and enthusiasm. In the next segment, which showed campaign stops from the next day, Mr. Gore was somewhere in the state of Michigan, which has a large number of union members. His comments were exactly the opposite and also met with great cheers of approval. I saw this with my own eyes and thought to myself "how does the man who claims to have invented the internet not understand how the modern technology of television works?"

This text does not permit the opportunity to get into all of the shenanigans that labor unions have perpetrated upon business in order to maintain their existence, but just know that while at one time in our history organized unions were a necessary and positive force, that time has long since passed. Now labor unions are a drag upon the American economy and a threat to a free and prosperous work force.

Voter ID Laws

Stemming from the concerted efforts of some primarily white southerners in the advent of abolition right up through the 1960's to circumvent federal law by restricting black voters through the use of deceptive and unfair practices within the registration and voting procedure, there is an understandable concern to ensure that every American, that is legally authorized to cast a ballot, can indeed vote.

After the Civil War ended in 1865, the Republican Congress passed the 13th Amendment to the Constitution abolishing slavery. Then, the 14th Amendment was passed to grant full civil rights to all free men. Southern states continued to resist allowing black men to vote which necessitated the passing of the 15th Amendment to explicitly give voting rights to black American men. At the time, there were 56 Democrats serving in Congress and not one of them voted for the 15th Amendment.

In the modern era, a different type of voting manipulation has taken place. Through the years, primarily in heavily populated urban areas, there have been shady practices involving either people being paid to show up representing themselves as another individual to cast a ballot, or even assuming the identity of a deceased person who is known to still be on the voter rolls in order to amass more votes for one candidate. During Democrat Mayor Richard Daly's tenure in Chicago, this phrase was often heard on Election Day "Vote early, and vote often." The Democratic Party has a long standing tradition of going into the black community and supplying the local ministers with "walking around" money. These funds were to be used to get their congregations to the polls.

Before computers and technology, the voting process was conducted either by hand or by some pretty primitive automation which still allowed for either human error or manipulation. Through the use of computers and technology instances of voter fraud have been greatly reduced...with one notable exception; voter ID fraud.

Voter ID fraud is another issue where the two parties positions are markedly different. In this country, it is nearly impossible to not possess a government-issued photo ID to prove you are who you say you are. Almost everyone has a driver's license, but for those who do not, a photo ID is available for either free or a nominal charge through the state government where you reside. All you have to do is prove your identity by providing a birth certificate or other acceptable identification. If you are disabled or a senior citizen, the local government will even come and pick you up and take you to the local office that issues these ID cards.

You need a photo ID for almost everything in this life. To drive, to fly, to receive government benefits, you even need a photo ID to get into the Democratic National Convention, but amazingly you do not need one to cast a ballot on Election Day.

In watching this debate take place on the cable talk shows, it almost appears that Democrats are trying to make the case that minorities are too stupid or incompetent to be able to obtain a legitimate ID.

Democrats are vehemently opposed to changing this, inciting the more than fifty year old history of the practices that did occur during desegregation and the civil rights movement. That was, quite simply, a different place and time. In the modern era, how can there possibly be anything wrong with requiring an individual to show a photo ID in order to cast their ballot? In my research, I have not found one verified case of an individual being refused the right to vote when they have complied with the jurisdictional requirements. On the contrary, our present day system bends over backwards to allow citizens the ability to exercise their constitutional right.

Republicans simply want to make sure that our laws are enforced and our elections are legitimate. There is though, a secondary reason why Republicans are behind the enactment of voter ID requirements. The reality is, that most people who are in this country illegally or are not otherwise allowed to vote (i.e. convicted felons), would vote for Democrats if given the opportunity.

This statement enrages many on the left, and understandably so...but it is true.

American Exceptionalism

The United States of America is truly an exceptional country. Look at all of the industry and technology we have spearheaded and created in less than two hundred fifty years of existence. Manned flight is outrageous enough, but we put a man on the moon. Phenomenal.

As Americans, we can take pride in so much more. No other country in the world has given as much economic and humanitarian aid to other countries as we have. Every year we spend billions and billions of dollars on aid to both existing and developing nations. We are known throughout the world as a bastion of freedom. Freedom from political, economic, and religious persecution. America, a place where you can live free and pursue your dreams. (This is one of the reasons why we have an illegal immigration problem.)

Despite all of this, you will encounter people who will tell you that America is an arrogant and selfish nation. A nation of self-importance and wealth. They will hold up other countries as examples and say "That's not how Germany does it" or France, or Italy. In reality, we don't want to be like those countries; many in those countries look down upon us because they are jealous. England, France, Spain, and Russia were all once world powers, but no more. There is but one super power nation in the world and thank God, it's the United States of America. Never feel guilty about that. We have earned this spot and with this power we have great responsibility. We have conducted ourselves accordingly.

American exceptionalism is one of the things that makes our country great, so don't ever apologize for that. We are the freest of the free and have produced the most prolific economic system the world has ever known, all while guaranteeing the rights of a free society.

Just ask yourself this question. Of all the countries in the world that have had to put up fences and other barriers to keep their people from leaving, which country is so prosperous and free that they have to put up barriers in order to keep people from entering illegally?

CHAPTER FIVE

NO GLOVE FITS PERFECTLY...

"Abortion should not only be safe and legal, it should be rare" - Bill Clinton

Some Things Conservatives Don't Understand

The basis of the formation of our country was the freedom of, and just as importantly, the freedom from religion. In the United States of America, individuals are free to observe and practice any religion of their choosing, including the right to worship no religion at all.

Some people are under the impression that freedom of religion does not mean freedom from religion. But think about it, when it comes to religion how could you ever truly have the freedom to believe in whatever you choose, if it didn't include the right to believe in nothing at all? For some people, that is their choice, therefore freedom of religion obviously includes freedom from religion.

It's unfortunate, but since the beginning of time organized religion has been the cause of more wars, violence, and death than any other force known to man. Look at the military conflicts going on in the world today and realize that most of them are disputes over religious beliefs and some of them have been going on for over two thousand years.

I point this out to illustrate what can happen when you so adamantly insist upon everyone else worshiping and believing in the same God that you do. This is the exact same thing that King James did in England that caused our forefathers to seek religious freedom in a new land. It's also the same thing that resulted in the genocide in Bosnia, the Holocaust in Germany, and the reason why we are fighting a "war on terror" against radical Muslims today. Millions and millions of people have been killed because of religious intolerance.

The subject of religion is where many conservatives get tripped up. It is true our nation was formed and our freedoms derived from our *God-given* right to exist and pursue happiness without fear of persecution. The Republican Party is deeply rooted as the party of "family values" and these beliefs are based primarily on one's faith in God and their desire to live their lives as the Bible has instructed them to.

We need to be careful however not to co-mingle our personal religious beliefs with our conservative doctrine. As Americans, we often fall victim to assuming that everyone does things our way. This is a legitimate criticism of us by the rest of the world. Even though our country was founded on *God-given* principles, it was also founded with the underlying freedom to observe and worship the religion of your choice, or no religion at all.

If you are not cognoscente of the importance of differentiating between these two aspects of your life, it will severely affect your ability to adopt a *true* conservative mindset and belief system.

For example:

It is a common theme these days to hear people say that one of our societal problems is that we have taken "God" out of the schools. Most people do not understand what the Constitution says about the separation of church and state. What the Constitution specifically says is that the government shall not sponsor or endorse a particular religion. Liberals have taken this to mean you cannot mention or even refer to "God" in school and that no religious activities can take place on a public school campus or facility within the constructs of receiving an education. They even go so far as to prevent members of a religious faith (let's say Christians) from gathering and sharing fellowship on campus. This, of course, is not what the Constitution refers to, as this is not in any way state sponsored. All religious groups on campus should have the right to gather among themselves and observe their common beliefs, without fear of offending anyone, or worse, being accused of violating the separation of church and state.

As ridiculous as some of the liberal beliefs on this subject are, unfortunately conservatives can fall victim to the same misinterpretation and misunderstanding of what is called for under our Constitution.

First of all, despite what you may have been told there has never been a law passed or Supreme Court ruling forbidding prayer in public school. You can go to school tomorrow and pray to the God of your choice all that you want.

An exercise that I occasionally enjoy is when gathered with a group that is discussing the ills of our current society; someone will inevitably say something to the effect of "We should get religion back in the schools. Everything started going to hell in a hand basket when we took God out of the schools," and everyone nods in agreement.

I then express surprise and ask "So you don't have a problem with your child being taught to follow the teachings of Judaism or how to worship Muhammad?" This is usually met with a look of bewilderment and what soon follows is the understanding that these individuals are actually only interested in putting religion back in schools as long as it's *their* religion that's taught. The thought never occurred to them that it would be anything else.

This same line of thinking jeopardizes a *true* conservatives belief on the "right to life" or abortion issue. This is a difficult issue to broach in a book aimed at a younger audience, but this issue, and more importantly the lack of proper under-standing of this issue, is so very important to the understanding of what it truly means to be a conservative. Furthermore, this issue has been grossly misrepresented, even lied about by the liberally biased media in our country, and has already cost us countless state, and most likely at least one national election.

First, let's get the terminology correct. An individual can either be "pro-life" which refers to being anti-abortion or "pro-choice" which refers to supporting a woman's right to choose what will ultimately occur with her body. Sometimes you will hear the pro-choice position inaccurately described as "pro-abortion." This is mean-spirited, because I can assure you that regardless of your thought processes, no one is "pro-abortion." To describe a person as "pro-abortion," who despite their personal beliefs or convictions has recognized that others do indeed possess the right to control what happens to their body, is reprehensible and intellectually dishonest.

This debate will rage for many years to come because in many ways it is quite literally the proverbial "chicken or the egg" debate. On this one there is no easy answer. Again, to be intellectually honest, one would have to admit that life does indeed begin at conception, but this cell mass cannot sustain itself outside of the mother's body for several months to come. A popular pro-life argument is that yes, it is a choice, a choice whether to engage in an activity that is known to cause pregnancy. Once you have made that choice, you have surrendered your "choice" on whether or not you can terminate a pregnancy.

On the other side, we have to go back to our conservative roots; an individual's right to pursue life, liberty, and happiness unfettered by government rules and regulations. Shouldn't all individuals be able to exercise judgment and control over what happens to their body? Should the government be able to dictate what are good choices and what are bad choices? Should the government be involved at all?

But then, at what point do the rights of an unborn individual become pertinent? Like I said, the chicken? Or the egg?

(Don't let yourself get bogged down in a debate over whether an abortion is only to be permitted in the cases of rape or incest. This is subterfuge meant to cloud the issue. We are talking about the formation of your ideology, either they are permissible, or they are not.)

In my opinion, in order to adhere to my core conservative beliefs, I have to be pro-choice. An abortion is an unfortunate act, and I am personally not in favor of them, but as a conservative, I could never seek to force my personal beliefs on another individual who did not share the same view point.

One of the things that I would have to agree with former President Bill Clinton on is that "abortion should not only be safe and legal, it should be rare."

Even though I am personally opposed to the practice, I do concede that there are times when this procedure is medically and practically necessary. It is not within my rights to interfere with the reproductive rights of another individual.

If you are to be a *true* conservative you can hold a deep personal conviction and live your life in accordance with that belief, while also defending the rights of others to make their own decisions. Either you are for personal responsibility, or you are not. It may not always be pretty.

The Fundamental Christian Right

America is a Christian nation; the majority of our citizens identify themselves as believing in some denomination of the Christian faith. There is a faction most commonly identified with the Republican Party referred to as the "Christian Right."

These folks are very vocal in their opposition to abortion, homosexuality, and other moral issues of today. While well meaning, they are a primary factor in why the Republican Party is seen as rigid and unyielding when it comes to debate and dialogue. They possess what can only be described as a "fundamental" religious mindset that includes a strict and literal interpretation of the Bible. These folks are the reason why in science class you are taught two theories on how the earth came to be. The fundamentalists' believe, as recounted in the book of Genesis, the earth was created by God in six days. From the scientific standpoint, you have learned about the "big bang theory" and the "primordial soup" from which the earth and its creatures have evolved. More recently, the term "intelligent design" has been offered up to represent the creation argument while attempting to blend in some scientific information.

A *true* conservative should defend the rights of all individuals to freely worship the religion of their choice, but should also defend against the manipulation of our political party in an effort to promote religious dogma. In considering whether we should allow fundamentalist Christians who interpret the Bible literally to dictate our party platform, please consider these points....

The Bible was not written by God or Jesus, it was written by men. The Bible was written hundreds of years after Jesus walked the earth. There were many religious writings of the time representing the newly established Christian religion but only a select few were chosen to be included in the Bible. Chosen by men, not God. Initially, these stories were handed down verbally through the years until eventually they were written down.

The Old Testament writings were originally recorded in Hebrew and then hundreds of years later translated into the English language. Unfortunately, there are many Hebrew words that do not have an exact translation into English, so the translators did the best that they could. The New Testament was translated from the original Greek language into English. In the early 1600's the King of England changed the Bible in an effort to unify different versions and to clean up some loose ends. Many of the Bibles today still bear the imprint "King James Version."

Based on these points, can you see how interpreting the Bible literally as "God's word" can lead to a manipulated view point?

Can you see how important it is as a conservative to adhere to our Constitution and not to an interpretation of Biblical prophecy?

This further reinforces why we must remain a nation of laws, not a nation of men. Men are fallible. Men can seek to alter or reinterpret meanings as to fit their beliefs or circumstances.

Racism vs. Prejudice vs. Bigotry

Racism will probably be the most misused word in the twenty-first century. Racism is the inherent belief in the superiority of one race over another. I know of very few people who actually believe this, though I have to admit there are probably some that do.

Prejudice is something we all practice, all races, all religions, etc. It would be impossible to not pre-judge people or situations on a daily basis. If you were in a neighborhood and you knew that seventy percent of the crime was committed by purple people and you found yourself walking down the street at night and encountered a purple person, you would pre-judge the situation, I don't care who you are.

Bigotry is what most people experience when they claim racism. Bigots know that they are not genetically superior to other races; they just don't like people who are different from them. They are very small-minded individuals. Through history bigotry has occurred over religion, race, and sexual preference... and it always will.

White conservatives that embrace bigoted or racist views and use racial slurs as part of their everyday vocabulary, make it so much more difficult for those that want to advance the conservative agenda based on facts and principles.

These people may hold what I believe are the correct political positions, but for the wrong reasons. Once a person uses the N-word, or it becomes obvious that their opinion is based purely on another's skin color, they lose all credibility, and lend credence to the much over blown charge of "racism" that distracts us from the truth we are trying to teach. These people can make valid points regarding the lack of logic found in most liberal arguments, only to have them completely negated by the demonstration of their shallow, small-minded bigotry toward others who do not look like them.

There are still bigots in this world and there always will be. They come in all shapes, sizes, and colors. To the extent that some are conservatives, they drastically hurt our cause by enabling the "race card" to be thrown when we are trying to have a discussion based on fact and logic.

CHAPTER SIX

A QUICK LESSON ON ECONOMICS

"The problem with Socialism is that eventually you will run out of other people's money" - Margaret Thatcher

There is a glaring flaw in the liberal economic argument: that is, how to stimulate and create a prosperous and continuing economy. From my conversations with liberals, they always approach the desired goal of increasing the buying power of the lower and middle class by taking money away from the producers in our society, the investors and job creators, by increasing income taxes and redistributing this money through social welfare and aid programs.

It is true that this action will, for a time, stimulate the economy. People spending money facilitates commerce, but that in and of itself, is not a reason to simply "give" it to the lower economic class. This liberal proposition of "taking from the rich to give to the poor" is not a self-sustaining solution. Essentially, you are penalizing the behavior that you want (productivity) and rewarding those that are not so inclined.

At some point, the productive individuals, seeing that the more they earn, the more they have to give up to the government through paying higher income taxes, will simply choose not to take the actions that will increase their income. Remember, they have almost certainly already reached some degree of wealth.

They understand that it is not worth their effort to put up 100% of the capital, take 100% of the risk, make 100% of the sacrifices of time away from their families, working weekends, whatever it takes to make the business opportunity successful, to then have the government come in and take 50% or 60% of every dollar.

If you think I'm being facetious in using these percentages, I'm not.

While the tax bracket percentage can change from time to time, here is an actual 2013 example of a self-employed individual whose household earns $150,000 per year and lives in a state that also has an income tax.

Example: 28% federal income tax rate, 6% state income tax rate, 15.3% self-employment tax rate = 49.3%. That is 49.3% in state and federal income taxes for a self-employed individual, and this is after all of the expenses of operating a business have to be paid. The top bracket rate is 60.3%.

Now you see why you hear so much about cutting taxes from the Republican Party. The top bracket gives up more than half of what they earned to the federal government, and again, this was after taking on all of the risk. How would you like to have a partner like that?

(For informational purposes the middle class pays a 15% federal income tax rate on income of up to $72,500.)

These are just income tax rates. This does not include other societal taxes we pay such as sales tax, property tax, fuel taxes, etc. So you can provide an incentive to the "producers" in our society by lowering their tax rates and allowing them to keep more of the money they earn or you can raise their tax rates and penalize them, thus providing a disincentive to expand their businesses and to work harder in order to earn more money.

When you reward the productive segment of the population you achieve a sustained stimulus that will feed upon itself and grow the economy into an even bigger pie, thereby increasing economic opportunity for everyone. You create office towers, shopping centers and housing units, manufacturing plants, and so much more. Then someone has to build, manage and maintain all of these ventures. These people then become consumers, stimulating the economy, and paying income taxes to the government. These people will also need grocery stores, drycleaners, banks, and any number of other service providers. They will need automobiles, refrigerators, washers and dryers. This creates more jobs, and more commerce, further stimulating the economy, and yes, more people paying income taxes to the government. This is the self-sustaining way to not only stimulate, but grow the economy while rewarding and promoting the behavior you want more of.

To simply take money from the more productive and give it to the less productive, will produce a limited economic stimulus. They certainly will spend this money on something, but once they do it's gone, a one-time event, and the only way for it to occur again is to take more money from the producers, who in time will decide it's not worth it to produce.

For some reason liberals think that if you allow a wealthy person to retain their money that it's then held in a "vacuum" and simply sits outside of the economy providing no economic benefits. This of course, is not true.

There are basically only four things that a wealthy person can *choose* to do with their money. All of them provide economic stimulus.

The first thing they may be inclined to do is to be

very conservative and simply hold it in the bank. This does not take the money out of the economy; the lending institution will then invest in the community by lending this money out to small and large business owners who will create more economic activity and commerce.

Second, the wealthy person may choose to invest directly by building a shopping center, an apartment complex, or any other number of things. Somebody has to build these investments, live and work in these investments; then someone has to service all of these new consumers and so on. This investment provides a tremendous boost to the economy and creates more taxpayers.

The third thing that a wealthy person could do with their money is to simply spend it. They could even be totally obnoxious with their spending. They could go out and buy an airplane, or a boat, a second home, third home, fourth home, fifth home, (any number of things that a liberal claims to find abhorrent while there are children starving in Africa.) But guess what? This would also be a huge stimulant to the economy. Someone has to build these planes, boats, and homes, someone has to produce the materials and the components they are comprised of, and then someone has to sell them, or finance them, or insure them. Someone then has to repair and maintain these assets. The people with these jobs have to have a place to live, a grocery store, a dry cleaner, a bank, etc.

To take the money away from these producers, and redistribute it to the middle class for an, at best, one shot economic stimulus into the economy is ridiculous and un-American. (Ironically, after a redistribution of this kind, the money spent by the recipients, will eventually, just end up right back in the hands of a "producer.")

The fourth thing a wealthy person can *choose* to do with their wealth? Give it away. If they do, it will have been their choice to do so, and it will be their choice of recipient. It's their money.

All of these actions create economic activity which then expands our economy. This is why lowering income tax rates on the "wealthy" actually increases the revenue (taxes) collected by the Treasury Department. On face value, it would seem that reducing the income tax rate, would result in a reduction of the revenue collected by the government.

This would be referred to as a *static* assessment; it assumes that everything else will remain the same. They take the same income figures and simply perform the calculation at a lower rate and get a reduced figure, but that's not what happens in the real world.

As we have just discussed, wealthy people are job creators whether they spend their money obnoxiously or simply leave it in the bank. Their money will be put to good use and serves to create jobs, expand the economy, stimulate commerce, and thereby increases the number of people paying income taxes.

This is called a *dynamic* assessment; it takes into consideration the stimulative effect that lower tax rates will have on the overall economy. This is how the revenues to the government actually rise when the income tax rate is decreased. Some may say, "but if the government collects more taxes it will also inject this money into the economy serving as an economic stimulus." This brings up two points...first, the government redistribution of this money has been shown to be a "one-shot" stimulus. The lower and middle classes will simply take this money and increase their disposable income, that is to say, spend the money, instead of saving it or investing it. Other government tax money redistributions include creating "work," not jobs, but work. If you pay a person to build a new road or sidewalk, that's a one-time deal, once the road or sidewalk is built, there's no more work. It's not a job, it's just work (temporary.)

The second point is the moral one; who deserves the right to determine how your money is spent? You or your government? After all, it's your money, you worked for it. You traded a portion of your life in exchange for it.

The liberals among us believe that the government knows how to spend your money better than you do. Once this is established, they then work to create government programs to alleviate the problems in society as they see them. This puts a drain on the government's resources causing the government to increase taxes in order to pay for all of this social welfare.

Another example of the unintended consequences of liberalism occurs when they successfully push for a hike in the minimum wage. First of all, the minimum wage is just that, it's for people that possess the minimum education, the minimum training and experience, the minimum skill level, and that want to put forth the minimum effort. The minimum wage was never meant to be a wage to raise one's family on. It is the minimum one can legally earn; typically students and others just coming into the work force will receive this on their way to becoming more experienced and therefore more valuable to their employer. It is meant to be a starting point.

Democrats are big champions of wanting to raise the minimum wage saying that it's so low you can't even support your family on it. So they have an easy answer, once again, it seems so simple. Let's just get the employer to pay a higher minimum wage and this will take care of the problem. (They really should offer some business classes in liberal arts colleges.)

This is what happens in the real world: The employer only has so much money available to spend on labor costs. If he has 10 employees and the government mandates that the minimum wage goes up, that means everyone's wages go up. The guy making $8/hour now increases to $10/hour, the guy making $10/hour, now increases to $12/hour, and so on. This increase in labor costs will most likely affect the cost of the goods and services provided causing prices to go up for the end user, the consumer. But even more of a reality is that a business that once employed 20 people will now have to cut the number of employees. Remember, the business owner's revenues didn't go up; they still have the same budget for labor but must now pay each employee more. The only way this can be done is by letting some employees go. Who will be fired? Most likely the ones that are the least valuable, the least skilled, and the ones that put forth the least effort. So liberals, trying to help the lowest income class by mandating that employers pay them more, have actually cost them their jobs.

This is why you need to be a deep thinker, a critical thinker. Don't be a reactionary thinker. Every action will have a consequence... what will the consequences be? Here's another example that illustrates the economic law of supply and demand while pointing out the perils of government intervention. During the aftermath of localized disasters such as tornadoes and hurricanes, liberals have decried the actions of motel owners and convenience store owners who knowing that their supply chains have been broken, adjust the cost of the commodities they have available to sell. Liberals scream about price gouging to the point that some state legislatures have enacted legislation prohibiting raising prices after a disaster has occurred. Once again, on face value this seems like the fair thing to do, but we cannot forget the attributes of our supply and demand economy. Let's take a look at how this scenario plays out in real life.

Take the motel owner that has ten rooms available. These rooms usually rent for $89/night. The interstate that runs by this motel is jammed up with people trying to get as far away from the disaster as possible, but at some point they will have to stop for the evening. In the liberals' world, raising the prices of the rooms would be price gouging and not allowed. As the families come in, they are quoted the price of $89/room, per night. The first car has a mother and father, a mother-in-law, and three kids. They take three rooms. The second car that pulls in consists of two families that are traveling together, two sets of parents, and two sets of three kids. Each of the parents want their own rooms to get some rest for the next day, and each set of kids want their own rooms, so they take four rooms for the night. The third car that pulls in has parents, grandparents, and three kids; they take the remaining three rooms. The motel is now full. Three car loads of people fleeing the disaster area have been accommodated.

If the free market was allowed to perform as it should, this is what would have happened. The motel owner understands that the interstate is full and the demand for hotel rooms will quickly exceed the available supply. He decides to raise the price of each room to $289/night. When the first three cars exit the interstate and come in seeking lodging, they will quickly determine that the $289 price per room is too expensive to get more than one room for the car load. This will leave an additional seven rooms available for more people to exit the interstate and find a room for the night.

The same thing happens if you use bottled water as the commodity. One convenience store operator has 100 bottles of water regularly priced at 89 cents. A cargo van of 10 people stopped in having just been on the road for four hours and not knowing how much longer they would be out there. At the price of 89 cents per bottle, they took them all. Had the shop owner been able to raise the price of the water to $3 per bottle (like at a sporting event), most likely these folks would have only purchased enough so that each person could have a couple each, thus leaving 80 additional bottles for the next fifty or so thirsty travelers to purchase.

For most people, it's hard to imagine what it's like after a natural disaster. Some people lose their entire homes and have to relocate for the many months it will take to rebuild. For others, their home is still inhabitable but in dire need of repair. One thing that almost always occurs is that the power goes off and cannot be turned on until all of the lines have been cleared and repaired. This can take days, weeks, or months. This makes the need for an auxiliary generator almost mandatory. Generators are needed to provide power in order to occupy these homes, or to provide power to run the pumps for removing water or making necessary repairs.

It used to be that a guy could go to a hardware store and buy a truck full of generators and take them to the storm area. For his trouble he may make an extra $500 per generator. The people in the affected region who did not go out and purchase these generators in advance would gladly welcome the availability of someone now bringing one to them in their time of need. But this doesn't happen as much anymore, the liberals have labeled this price gauging and now the people who need these items the most will have to do without.

As you can see, the easiest or most simple answer is not always the best when it comes to more complex issues. Try and remember to think with your head instead of your heart. This does not make you a callous individual. In the long run you will be helping more people and helping those in need for a much longer period of time.

WHY YOUR FATHER'S A REPUBLICAN

CHAPTER 7

2012 CAMPAIGN ISSUES

"If you've got a business- you didn't build that- somebody else made that happen" - Barack Obama

There were many issues that comprised the campaign dialogue between President Barack Obama and Republican Nominee Willard "Mitt" Romney. In this chapter, I'll touch on most of the major issues in a heated campaign that was full of partisan mudslinging and media bias. There was even a debate moderated by a CNN anchor person who interjected herself into the fray by incorrectly siding with one candidate while breaking the momentum of the other on the subject of the terror attack in Benghazi that occurred on September 11, 2012 killing a U.S. Ambassador and three other Americans.

History will undoubtedly show how a biased and unquestioning media helped to distort facts, advance untruths, and even helped to perpetuate the cover up of an international terrorist incident until after the election had been decided.

Illegal Immigration

We hear so much about the immigration issue in the news and it has become an integral issue in our political elections. It is often reported in the media as the immigration debate and rarely correctly referenced as the *illegal* immigration debate. The debate is not over immigration, it's over illegal immigration. When you hear a liberal say "we are a nation of immigrants" in an effort to justify their position on the debate, remember they are misrepresenting the argument. We are a nation of *legal* immigrants. Our country, like most others, needs to control and be aware of who crosses our borders. This has always been important but never as important as after the attacks of 9/11/01.

Security is a real issue along our border with Mexico. Our southwestern states suffer from a severe lack of safety and an increased rate of crime and violence because of the lack of commitment to enforcing U.S. laws that are already on the books regarding illegal immigration. Democratic administrations do this to curry favor with the Latino voters. During this most recent election cycle, the state of Arizona was made a scapegoat and unscrupulously represented as a bigoted and racist state for passing legislation to protect their borders and deal with those who chose to enter our country illegally. The Governor and State Legislators were compared to Hitler and accused of using Gestapo-like tactics to enforce these laws. The news media readily bought into this argument and helped to repeat it enough so that low information voters and those who are ideologically challenged believed it.

What really happened was the state of Arizona grew tired of sending their tax money to Washington only to be told that our Nation's immigration laws would not be enforced to provide better border security. In response, Arizona decided to pass a state law that contained the same provisions as our federal law but also gave state officers permission to enforce these provisions. For this, the state was branded as racist, denounced by our President as intolerant, and subsequently sued by the U.S. Department of Justice led by Attorney General Eric Holder.

The immigration debate is comprised of two different issues: how to allow in those who wish to enter our country legally and how to handle those already in our country illegally. If you have a leaking roof you would first want to stop the leak by repairing how the water is coming in, then you would need to figure out how to remove the water that has flooded your home. The same is true for the debate on illegal immigration.

First, some history on the subject: In 1986 our country found itself in a similar situation regarding immigrants who had entered our country illegally. Thanks in great part to President Reagan (R) and supply-side economics our economy was booming and so prosperous that millions of people had entered our country seeking a better life, in search of the American dream. The debate focused on many of the same aspects as our debate today. What to do with those already here? The number of illegal immigrants was so enormous that any type of deportation or containment seemed fruitless. At the same time, how could we prevent this from becoming an ongoing problem, or occurring again in the future? As a result, President Reagan approved a one-time amnesty which allowed three million immigrants already here illegally to stay, as long as they were registered, so that we knew who was here. Having approved this measure, it was made clear this would be a one-time occurrence and measures would subsequently need to be put in place to restrict this kind of un-authorized access into our country. Congress failed to act. These measures never took place.

Ronald Reagan was a Republican and Republicans are not against immigration. We are against *illegal* immigration and all of the problems it brings our country from an economic standpoint as well as a security standpoint. Republicans remember what occurred in 1986 (a one-time forgiveness in an effort to fix the illegal immigration problem once and for all) and on 9/11/2001 (a horrible act of terrorism perpetrated against us in part due to our lax immigration monitoring) and we do not wish to see a repeat of either.

Another societal irony is that most immigrants to this country are traditionally aligned with conservative values. They are religious, family oriented, hard-working individuals. They want nothing from government except for it to stay out of their way and allow a level playing field for them to prosper. These are all attributes of the Republican Party. The irony is that since the Democratic Party knows that many immigrants are here illegally, or have family members that are here illegally, or have family members back in their home country they wish to bring here, they pander to this group of voters knowing they will most likely vote Democratic because of this one issue. Additionally, the Republican Party has not done a good job in creating a response to erroneous Democratic claims and continues to let the media define its position.

In the election of 2012, our nominee Mitt Romney unfortunately had it wrong. His sense of fairness compelled him to propose that immigrants here illegally, "self deport," leave our country and go to the back of the line. This certainly would have been fair, but terribly impractical, and certainly not what the millions of illegal aliens and those legally here who wished to bring their family members in, wanted to hear.

A key component to become a legal immigrant entering this country is to be law-abiding. If an immigrant enters this country without following our procedures, they have done so illegally. When they then earn income without paying taxes, they have done so illegally. When they drive, they operate a vehicle without a license and without insurance, which are both illegal. This illegal foundation is not what we are looking for in our immigrant population. To say nothing of the fact that millions of people are still on the waiting list to gain entry to this country and become legal citizens. Our system of law and fairness, along with American Exceptionalism are all reasons why these immigrants want to come to our country in the first place. Certainly they can appreciate our need for enforcing our immigration laws, can't they? As with most things in life, there is a right way and a wrong way to do things. Entering our country illegally is the wrong way.

The War on Women

One of the more outrageous claims that Democrats concocted during the 2012 election cycle was that the Republican Party had declared a "war on women."

In order to discuss the "war on women" issue, we

must first remind ourselves what the meaning of religious freedom is and that as Americans we have the right not to have our religious beliefs dictated to us by our government. Furthermore, we also have the right not to have the government force us to participate in activities or practices that are in direct conflict to our religious beliefs.

As we have discussed in previous chapters, in order to be a *true* conservative, you must be able to separate your conservative view points from your religious beliefs, and realize that they can co-exist. It doesn't matter how much you may personally disagree with an act or behavior, if it meets the lawful or constitutional test, another individual does have the right to engage in such acts or behaviors.

The right of an individual to have the ultimate control over their body and what they do with their body is one of these acts and behaviors. We are talking about a woman's right to choose to terminate a pregnancy. Not a pleasant subject, but if you truly believe in the rights of the individual, you must believe in acknowledging that this right exists.

Having said this, if you personally disagree with these acts, or if they violate your religious beliefs, should your money be used to pay for these procedures? Does it violate your constitutional rights to have the government take your tax dollars from you by force and require that they be used to support organizations that provide these services?

As a nation we recognized shortly after Roe v Wade (U.S. Supreme Court decision legalizing abortion) that there should be no direct government funding of abortions. The Hyde Amendment from 1977 makes it illegal to use federal (tax payer) funds for this purpose. The Democrats however have gotten around this rule by funding family planning organizations that also promote and provide these procedures.

Every year, millions of Americans have their tax dollars used to provide contraceptive and reproductive services to women for activities and procedures that are in direct conflict with their religious convictions.

For some reason, liberals cannot recognize that there are two separate issues here. Just because someone has the right to do something does not create an obligation for the government to pay for or provide it. Making matters worse, the government is using tax dollars collected from individuals who expressly disapprove of these acts. It seems liberals can recognize the denial of a person's rights on the one hand, but not the other.

This is what the perceived "war on women" issue

revolves around. Democrats insist that since a woman has the right to choose, that your tax dollars must be used to fund abortions and birth control. Even if your religion tells you these practices are wrong.

It is true that a long standing tenant of the conservative platform is to overturn the Supreme Court ruling that made abortions legal in our country (Roe v Wade), but this will never happen, and more and more conservatives are accepting of this.

The Democrats however continue to demagogue this issue. They distort the facts and then play upon the emotions of the people who believe the distortion. Republicans are actively trying to de-fund organizations like Planned Parenthood (the largest provider of abortions in the country) who receive our federal tax dollars while also promoting and funding these procedures. In 2011, U.S. Congressman Mike Pence from Indiana introduced house bill HR 217 to accomplish this, arguing that it is "morally wrong to take the tax dollars of millions of pro-life Americans and use them to fund organizations that provide and promote abortions." He was 100% correct.

Liberals simply cannot make the distinction between these two arguments. During the 2012 election campaign, Democrats falsely claimed that this legislation was aimed at reversing Roe v Wade and constituted a "war on women" by seeking to eliminate their right to choose. The issue, of course, was not a woman's right to choose, it was making taxpayers pay for these procedures.

Republicans tried to correctly state the argument but were drowned out by liberal activists and denied the right of clarification by the news media.

Liberal bullying tactics are so egregious that also in 2012 when a private organization, The Susan G. Komen for the Cure cancer charity decided they would no longer provide funding to Planned Parenthood because the organization was under a federal criminal investigation, the backlash (by people who refused to acknowledge the true issue) was so fierce that Komen reversed its decision after just a couple of days.

The Komen organization had long been considering withdrawing funding from Planned Parenthood because one of their services was promoting and providing abortions. Komen's specific purpose in funding Planned Parenthood was exclusively for their breast cancer screening services.

In the end, Komen was bullied by abortion advocates who threatened to boycott Komen's "Walk for the Cure" and other fundraising activities, all while mounting an intimidation campaign against them in the media. This defunding decision was made by a private organization. Shouldn't they be allowed to set their own guidelines and decide which organizations they will provide funding for? If you don't agree with their position, then don't contribute to them. But don't try to end their existence by misstating their position and bullying them into accepting yours.

Another reason for the creation of the false assertion there was a "war on women" was the adoption of a national health care law that was passed by Democrats in 2010. Through the process of implementation, it was discovered that one of the requirements of this legislation was for employers to include birth control coverage in their company provided health plans. So here again, we have the issue of the government mandating that an employer, who may be opposed to such means of contraception on religious or moral grounds, was being required to provide it to their employees. Even more ridiculous are the instances where the employer was a religious institution, such as the Catholic Church, who actively denounced such contraception methods. They too were being forced to provide this *benefit* that was in direct violation of their religious teachings. (After much public backlash from the Catholic Church and other religious organizations, an exemption was eventually provided, allowing an insured of a religious employer to be able to deal directly with the insurer and receive these products at no additional charge.)

Republicans simply wanted to right this wrong but were repeatedly shouted down with the mischaracterization of their argument by Democratic spokespeople and the news media.

The liberal argument, that Republicans wanted to deny women the right to reproductive health care, was shouted so loudly and repeated so often, that many low information voters ultimately believed it. The news media actively used the phrase "Republican War on Women" when reporting the evening news. Then, as now, there was no Republican War on Women.

Social Security Reform

Again and unfortunately, the Republicans have done a horrible job in communicating their position on Social Security. The Democrats also do an excellent job misrepresenting the argument.

All that senior citizens that depend on Social Security income for all, or a good part of their retirement hear is that the Republicans want to take some of their social security benefits away.

What they don't hear is that the Social Security program is actually insolvent; that's a nice way of saying it is broke. There is no Social Security lock box that pays these benefits to seniors. In 1968, President Lyndon Johnson (D) and the Democrats passed legislation that allowed them to use the money people paid into Social Security as part of the general budget. In return they would put government IOUs in the Social Security lock box. Now all we have in there are IOUs. Given the age of today's senior citizens you would think they would remember when this occurred, but for some reason they don't.

So now, Social Security is broke and depends on the money that younger taxpayers pay into the system to pay benefits out to today's seniors. Yes, if private enterprise had concocted a scheme like this they would be in prison right now. In the rest of the world this is called a Ponzi scheme.

Republicans are simply pointing out that something needs to be done to reform this program to continue its viability for future generations that are presently paying into it. Today, most young people do not believe that the Social Security program will be around for them when they retire, even though they are having money deducted for it from their paycheck every pay period. The Democrats use the Republican position of wanting to reform the Social Security system to mislead seniors and claim that Republicans want to reduce their benefits, and thus their monthly check.

The system has become unsustainable; the average recipient today receives about three times the amount they have paid into the system. But that's okay, because our government promised them these benefits and we need to live up to that promise. We also need to reform this system or it will fail. Presently it takes about six new contributors to Social Security to pay the entitlement for each retired recipient. This simply cannot continue.

The Forty-Seven Percent

"There are forty-seven percent of the people who will vote for the President no matter what. All right, there are forty-seven percent that are with him, who are dependent on government, who believe that they are victims, who believe the government has a responsibility to take care of them, who believe that they are entitled to health care, to food, to housing, to you name it. That, that's an entitlement, and the government should give it to them. And they will vote for this president no matter what." - Mitt Romney.

Mr. Romney went on to say that "My job is not to worry about these people ... I'll never convince them they should take personal responsibility and care for their lives."

Mr. Romney said this at a private Florida fundraising event. Someone secretly videotaped his comments and posted them on You Tube. When confronted with the remarks, Mr. Romney acknowledged he had made them and stuck to his words, although acknowledging he could have been more "eloquent." As you can imagine, the Left picked up this ball and ran with it. Using it to, in their words, show that Mitt Romney doesn't care about you, he just cares about his rich friends; he's not going to be your President.

Let's put Mr. Romney's comments into context. This was Candidate Romney, who was speaking about his campaign strategy, how he would win the election. The financial supporters he was speaking to wanted to know how their contributions were going to be spent. Obviously, if you already knew, because it had already been reported, that forty-seven percent of the electorate was not going to vote for you, no matter what, it would be foolish to waste any time, money, or other resources in an effort to gain their vote. It would truly be a waste of time; Mr. Romney was simply acknowledging this.

What he said was true: if you were a supporter of President Obama you most likely believe that the government has the obligation to provide our citizens with healthcare, food, and housing. This is what the Democrats stand for. So, Mr. Romney's message of economic growth and lower income taxes would mean nothing to people who depend on the government for these "entitlements."

As I have mentioned earlier in this book, entitlements used to mean programs that people had paid into and would expect to receive a benefit from, they would be entitled to it. If the government required you to have money withheld from your paycheck in order to contribute to the Social Security program, you would then be entitled to receive Social Security benefits when you become eligible for the program. If the government offered you a guaranteed medical benefit for the rest of your life as an incentive to join our military forces, then after you were discharged you would be entitled to this medical care for life. This is what used to be known as an entitlement. You contributed to the program in order to receive a benefit. Today however, apparently to make it harder to debate this topic, welfare benefits such as Section 8 housing, food stamps, the WIC program, and many other forms of government support are now lumped in with and referred to as entitlements, even though these people have not contributed to these programs. They are paid for by our tax dollars. So I ask again, could referring to these programs as entitlements be the reason why so many Americans feel they are entitled to receive free housing, free food, and a free check for the other expenses they incur in life?

The truth is Mr. Romney's statement was 100% correct. The real battle for the Presidency was over the "undecided" voters estimated to be somewhere around six percent of the voting population. Knowing this, why would you devote any resources to the 47% that will not vote for you regardless? The answer of course is that you wouldn't. Don't let someone else explain this to you, if you are interested, find a complete unedited version of this video and listen to the question and the answer. Clearly Mr. Romney is not saying if elected he would not care about forty-seven percent of American citizens.

Note: It became known that the person who helped leak this video to the press was the grandson of former President Jimmy Carter. Attempting to bring someone else down in an effort to make your position look better is not the right thing to do. Stick to the high road and let the unfiltered and in context facts speak for themselves. If you have to distort someone's position in an effort to win the debate, you are most likely on the wrong side.

Warren Buffet Pays a Lower Income Tax Rate than His Secretary

Billionaire Warren Buffet is admired by many for his creation of an amazing financial portfolio. I have always been a big fan of Mr. Buffet and his American success story really is quite amazing.

During the 2012 campaign, the Democratic Party resurrected a quote from Mr. Buffet where he decried the fact that as a multi-billionaire he pays a lower income tax rate than his secretary.

This quote was picked up and ran with by every liberal available including the one running for re-election to the Presidency. It was referred to during every debate and discussion on whether the rich pay their fair share of taxes. Unfortunately, this quote has caused many conservatives including myself to lose the great respect and admiration we had for Mr. Buffet. Here's why...

This statement is intellectually dishonest. Mr. Buffet and his secretary derive their income in two different ways. Mr. Buffet's income is derived from capital gains earnings and therefore taxed at a lower rate than ordinary income, which is how his secretary's income is derived. Who set up Mr. Buffet's compensation to minimize his tax obligation? Mr. Buffet did.

What's worse is that since Mr. Buffet is a very smart man, he understands this difference. He also understands that when many low-information voters hear that he said that he pays a lower tax rate than his secretary, what they think they hear is that Warren Buffet said his secretary (making a reported $60,000 a year) pays more in income taxes than he does. Of course, this isn't true. Mr. Buffet while paying a lower effective rate because of the way he set up his compensation still pays millions and millions of dollars in income taxes every year. Mr. Buffet surely knows that this is the kind of misleading information that promotes the class warfare that threatens to ruin our great nation. If Mr. Buffet feels he should be paying more in income taxes then he should restructure his compensation plan so that more of it can be counted as ordinary earned income.

While disappointing to me, this should serve as a shining example to not believe everything you hear, and to not simply take it at face value. Look into it for yourself and examine the validity of the statement. Apparently even the most brilliant among us can fall victim to using fuzzy math and intellectual dishonesty when promoting a cause that we believe in.

Obamacare

In 2010 Congress voted to enact legislation

proposed by President Obama entitled The Patient Protection and Affordable Care Act, more commonly referred to as "Obamacare."

The intricacies of how and why health care and therefore health insurance is far more expensive than it should be is too great of a discussion to get into in this text. Suffice it to say, the government's involvement in healthcare through Medicare and Medicaid and our legal system's failure to reign in both frivolous lawsuits and ridiculous civil judgment amounts via tort reform are two major contributors.

Obamacare does a lot of things, the bill itself was over 2700 pages long and truthfully not even the lawmakers who passed it knew everything it contained. Again, this legislation and its implications are far too detailed and require such a great amount of education on the subject to have a fruitful discussion, I simply cannot cover it here. At its core, the base argument was whether the federal government could require an individual to purchase a product or service, in this case health insurance.

Conservatives insist this requirement infringes upon an individual's right to govern their own affairs and that as such it was unconstitutional. Liberals with their belief that the federal government should act as a "nanny state" and take care of everyone, even against their own will and desire, were advocates of the law.

The true issue at hand was the cost of health insurance. A fact missed by many is the reason health insurance is so expensive is because the underlying commodity that it covers, health care, is so expensive. Obamacare does nothing to reduce the cost of health insurance for most individuals; it actually makes it more expensive, and then makes you pay a penalty if you do not purchase it.

While the majority of Americans have never been in favor of Obamacare, Democrats were successful in convincing their constituents that this legislation would either make health insurance affordable for them, or provide it to them for free.

This did not help the Republicans in the election of 2012, but as we approach 2014 when Obamacare is set for full implementation we can already see the effects of this flawed "utopian" legislation.

In the end this will turn out to be an effort pushed upon the American people by a President during his first term in office at the expense of working on so many other important issues of the day, including what was needed most, the economy. I truly believe we will look back at this legislation and realize that with its implementation, its failure to perform as promised, and its deconstruction and phase out, we will have wasted eight to ten years of valuable time and resources.

Blue States vs. Red States

During election years the political majority maps are illustrated using either "blue" for Democratic Party controlled states or "red" for Republican majority states.

In 2013, the Mercatus Center of George Mason University published a study entitled "Freedom in the 50 States." The study measured economic and personal freedom using various criteria that included tax rate, regulatory burden, unions, gun control, and more.

The study found that not only do the most free states tend to be "red" states (majority Republican) but that American "net" migration between states seems to be overwhelmingly from "blue" to "red." Meaning that people are moving from "blue" states where freedom is more regulated, to "red" states where more freedom can be found. The study also showed that economic growth was higher in the "red" states since they offered lower taxes and less regulatory burdens for companies to deal with.

So much for the presidential campaign trail rhetoric that lower taxes and less regulation will not help our economy grow. President Obama was fond of saying "They tell us, if we just cut more regulations and cut more taxes, especially for the wealthy, our economy will grow stronger. Here's the problem. It doesn't work. It has never worked."

Just because someone looks you in the eye, with a glimmer in his, changes the natural cadence in which he speaks, and tells you something is true, does not make it so.

WHY YOUR FATHER'S A REPUBLICAN

CHAPTER EIGHT

CONCLUSION-MOVING FORWARD

"Swing voters are more appropriately known as the 'idiot voters' because they have no set of philosophical principles. By the age of fourteen, you're either a Conservative or a Liberal if you have an IQ above a toaster." – Ann Coulter

Real Political Correctness

In recent years I have been a part of a crowd that refers to Democrats as being members of the Democrat Party. After all, if you are a Republican you are a member of the Republican Party, it then only makes sense that if you are a Democrat, you are a member of the Democrat Party. It sounds awkward to refer to someone as a member of the "Democratic" party; it seems to be more of a verb than a noun.

I also understand that some low information voters may erroneously equate the "Democratic" Party with our "democratic" system of government and decide that this must be the correct party to align themselves with.

For these reasons, several years ago, I began using

the term "Democrat" Party in an effort to be grammatically correct. In the process of writing this book, I decided to research this issue. It turns out that I am not the only one who has felt this way over the years but even so, the correct name of the party as it was founded is the "Democratic" Party. This is how it should appear in news articles and on voting ballots. Therefore I will do my best to discontinue the use of the term "Democrat" when referring to the political party.

Abortion and Gay Marriage

The *Christian Right* will not appreciate the positions I put forth on abortion and gay marriage, but you have to realize their opposition is exactly why *true* conservatives need to separate their religious beliefs from their political viewpoints.

In the United States of America, a free thinking political party must base their platform on the "God-given" individual rights given to all of us in the U.S. Constitution. The affirmation they are "God-given" rights refers to the fact that no man can take them away.

It is very hard for many of us to separate our Christian religious values from our conservative political ones, but this must be done. This doesn't mean you now have to endorse abortion or gay marriage. Quite the contrary, stand up for what you believe in, but you cannot stand for denying another individual's right to live their life as they see fit. These two are not mutually exclusive. You can abhor abortion and also consider that in your religion *marriage* is between a man and a woman, and you can live your life in accordance with these principles.

Liberals must also learn to embrace this position. The politics of vilifying someone because they hold a different belief than you do must stop. Liberals will have to learn to accept that acknowledging a person's right to do something is all that is required. If their objective is for conservatives to accept and encourage these acts, they will never get there. If however, their objective is for conservatives to acknowledge that while it may not be right for them, an individual must not be denied their right to make these lifestyle choices, this is achievable.

I for one, was quite happy with simply allowing two people of the same sex who wished to be "married" be allowed to enter into a "civil union" recognized by the government so that they could extend their employment and retirement benefits to one another along with all the other formalities granted to traditional married couples. I did not see the need to call it marriage. For me, marriage is a religious term and most if not all religions do not condone same sex marriages. For a long time, I believed in my heart, that this should be enough, allow for everything else but, let's not call this "marriage."

Then, after several years and specifically when this became a major issue in the presidential elections, I decided to re-examine this in the same way I examine other issues of rights and fairness. I do this by essentially putting the shoe on the other foot and see if the argument still holds up. When it comes to discussing individual liberties and rights, you should be able to change the parties involved around and still agree with the outcome of the statement. For instance, if you believe that religion should be put back into public schools. Which religion? The Christian religion, of course. Okay, now swap the word Christian with the word Jewish, or Muslim, or Hindu. Can you still agree with the statement? If not, it must mean that Christian is not acceptable either. It only works from your standpoint but not from the standpoint of others.

Again, it is so important that you realize no one is discouraging you from being a Christian or a practicing member of any other faith that you choose, but these religious convictions cannot be the basis for the creation and interpretation of our laws. You must be able to separate the two or you will never truly understand what is meant by individual freedom. Individual freedom is not just for you, it's for everybody.

For over one hundred years the Supreme Court of the United States has ruled that marriage is a fundamental right afforded the citizens of the United States, all of the citizens. In 1967, the Supreme Court overturned laws in twelve states that prohibited interracial marriages. In their decision, they affirmed the rights of all citizens to marry and condemned the notion that the "state" could dictate which Americans were to be afforded this right. At that time, in those states, interracial marriage just did not seem right. It went against nature, but in order to be fair to everyone a law must be able to pass the "shoe on the other foot" litmus test. The prohibition of marriage between races just didn't do that.

To me, same sex marriage seems unnatural and just doesn't feel right, because it's not right...for me. I firmly believed I was allowing for the same rights for all by accepting the "civil union" compromise. But in 2012 something about this was bugging me and I decided to re-examine the issue. I tried very hard to reason and explain that a distinction between same sex and heterosexual marriage could and should be made. Every reason I could come up with seemed to be biblically or religious based and I knew that in order for my position to be correct it must be able to stand up absent that basis. Just because a law or practice is religiously based does not make it unconstitutional (most of our laws are religiously based), but it must be able to meet the "fair to everyone involved" test outside of a religious context.

An individual must possess the freedom to marry the person they choose, free from government discrimination. It should not matter what your religion says, remember you can still personally oppose this, but you cannot take away a constitutional right from another citizen. It also should not matter what public opinion or the majority wants. This is why we are not a true democracy; we are a nation of laws that are meant to be applied to everyone equally.

In this country it is illegal to discriminate based on race, creed, color, sex, national origin, or sexual preference, so how can we, from a legal stand point, not allow gay marriage?

Be Prepared For the Lack of Logical Thinking and Obfuscation

The reason that conservatives and liberals disagree so often is because liberals *simply* think differently. Liberals, I believe, are more trusting, conservatives are more realistic.

Sometimes it's more a matter of logic; take for example Pulitzer Prize winning *New York Times* journalist Fox Butterfield. As often pointed out by *Wall Street Journal* editorial writer James Taranto, in 1997 Mr. Butterfield wrote an article titled "More Inmates, Despite Drop In Crime." Mr. Butterfield thought he was expressing a paradox while reporting that recently released statistics showed that crime was on the decrease while asking "So why is the number of inmates in prisons and jails around the nation still going up?" In 2004 Mr. Butterfield reiterates his perplexed state with "The number of inmates in state and federal prisons rose 2.1% last year, even as violent crime and property crime fell." Mr. Butterfield seems absolutely oblivious to the fact that the decrease in the amount of crimes being committed is a direct result of the increase in the country's prison population.

Mr. Butterfield is asserting a paradox where in reality a cause and effect relationship exists. Liberals *simply* think differently.

This supposed paradox is again asserted in a *Christian Science Monitor* article published on May 8, 2013. The article titled "With gun violence down, is America arming against an imagined threat?" The author presents a paradox between the increase in Americans arming themselves while an increase in gun violence is only "perceived" because of the over reporting of gun violence by the media. In reality the statistics show gun violence has decreased. This article accurately reports that the liberal myth of "more guns, more crime" is dispelled with this data, but again calls the data a "paradox" rather than a cause and effect relationship. The fact that crime rates are down is directly related to the fact that private, individual, gun ownership rates have risen. There's no paradox here.

You will however encounter many liberals that have absolutely no use for the facts. You can refute their positions all day long and expose the inaccuracies they have used to form their beliefs, and they will *never* care.

Liberals didn't decide to become liberal by using logic, they are liberals because they just know it's the right position to hold, they feel it in their heart. Either their family has always been liberal, or when they look around, all of the people they consider to be like them are liberal, or after learning certain utopian principles in school they ceased to continue the learning process and failed to adjust their viewpoints based on what they saw in the world around them. Some will simply vote for the party that will give them the most *stuff*.

When liberals cannot rely on the facts in an argument they will often seek to cloud the issue, either claiming racism, or seeking to perpetuate class warfare. If you watch the cable channel political talk shows where they pit liberal vs. conservative, you'll see that they basically devolve into "shout fests" with one side simply trying to shout down the other. If they are allowed to carry on a discussion however, note how the liberal will typically change the premise of the question in order to not answer it as asked, or they will simply start talking about what George W. Bush did while he was President. The shows that are hosted or moderated by liberals will often ask a question that has an incorrect premise in order to confuse the issue or prevent the conservative speaker from being able to address the true issue at hand.

Be prepared for these tactics as they account for about eighty percent of what you will be dealing with. In a fair debate, you will generally have the upper hand. The liberal argument suffers from a lack of logic. The same people who argue against the death penalty on the basis that it is cruel and unusual punishment have absolutely no problem supporting abortion. In the fight to end poverty, liberals offer incentives that reward (encourage) the behavior they are seeking less of, and in the war against crime and violence, liberals would prefer that we disarm law-abiding citizens.

Agree to Disagree

I hope from all that we have talked about in this book you agree that it is important to analyze why people think what they think, how they have developed their opinions, and how biased or incorrect information may have influenced these opinions.

While it's true that there are stereotypical mindsets that say rich white guys are conservative Republicans and minorities are always going to be liberal Democrats, in the real world, it's not always that way.

When I was three or four years old I went trick-or-treating with a young man who went on to become a major Hollywood movie star. This guy has reached the pinnacle of success in his field. We are the same race, the same general religion, about the same age, and we were raised in the same part of the country. There were differences, his up-bringing was a bit more privileged than mine, but overall I would say we had a lot in common. This gentleman grew up to become a notable liberal figure among the Hollywood elite. So much so I have heard he has shared texts and pick-up basketball games with the President of the United States. Why has he turned out to be a liberal while I turned out to be a conservative? Is it the Hollywood influence? Does he feel guilty about making a bazillion dollars pretending to be other people while reading words that others have written for him? I don't know.

I was in junior high school during the presidential election of 1976 when President Gerald Ford was running against Jimmy Carter. Our school held a mock debate that was broadcast over the intercom system. A student who was a supporter of each candidate was chosen to represent the already publicized views of the candidates. When the debate began, the announcement was made who the students would be portraying, then they themselves were immediately recognized by their voices.

The voice of Jimmy Carter was a kid who lived in my neighborhood. I immediately thought to myself "How could this guy be a Democrat?" All of my family was Republican. I thought everyone in our neighborhood was a Republican. How could this be? It was at that point when I was fourteen years old that I realized even though someone looks like you, comes from the same place as you, and has shared the same experiences, it doesn't mean they think just like you. I remember being stunned by this realization at the time and today, I continue to be fascinated, and am greatly intrigued, as to the reasons and thought processes that go into these differences of opinion.

(In fairness to this kid, he was only fourteen at the time. He, like myself, showed a very strong work ethic, both of us jumping into the work force as soon as legally possible, actually even before. I haven't seen or heard anything about him in over thirty years but I would bet a hundred bucks this kid is a Republican today.)

Just as every coin has two sides, some people will simply be liberal and some will simply be conservative. Statistically speaking, more men are conservative and more women are liberal.

You may find yourself to be more liberal on social issues and more conservative on fiscal issues. The important thing is to make a fully informed decision. Whatever you ultimately choose to believe is up to you. That is one of the truly exceptional freedoms that Americans have.

While it is important to form and be aware of your own political philosophy (so you can exercise your right to vote correctly), it is not something that you want to lose friendships or relationships over. You will have many friends who are of the opposite political persuasion but you will have many common interests when it comes to sports, music, movies and lots of other subjects. You will need to learn to be tolerant of others' viewpoints, which is sometimes easier said than done, and you will want to be mindful not to be the one who tortures others with your sincere beliefs. Like my wife always tells me "You can disagree, without being disagreeable."

So please, it is my sincere hope that you will use this book to simply help you make an informed decision as to which political philosophy that you will prescribe to, a tool to help you evaluate each of them.

If after reading this book you come away and can confidently identify yourself as a liberal Democrat, or as a conservative Republican, then this book has served its purpose. The most unfortunate situation I can imagine is for people to declare themselves one or the other, and to have done so as a result of being uninformed or misinformed.

When examining opposing viewpoints, consider where the individual has gained his or her knowledge and information from. Are they simply echoing beliefs they hear at home or going along with the crowd so they do not stand out? Sometimes for teenagers, being popular outweighs being correct. Always remember you are a "free thinking individual," be careful of falling victim to "group think."

At the end of the day, the most important thing is that you make an honest and sincere decision. If someone identifies themself as a member of a political party other than your own, and they have come to that conclusion honestly, and accurately, there is absolutely nothing wrong with that. You will simply have to agree to disagree and move on.

Consequences and Adjustments

The election of 2008 was an example of "smoke and mirrors" and a "grand illusion." The epitome of being told one thing, being sold a bill of goods, having been made promises that would never come to fruition, these promises probably made without the intention of ever being fulfilled. The election of 2008 is an example that sometimes "smoke and mirrors" works; people want to believe so badly, they just let emotion take the place of common sense. People are inclined to believe what they want to hear. What they want to hear is not always what they need to hear, what they want to hear is not always the truth.

Sometimes "smoke and mirrors" does win. The problem is you then get too far down the road before you realize it was just "smoke and mirrors." It was just wishful thinking and empty promises. You get so far down the road that you have to endure life altering consequences because you simply heard what you wanted to hear and didn't question the source or its accuracy.

The 2012 election was an example of the Republican Party letting its opponents define their positions for them. (The obvious bias of the mainstream media didn't help either.) That, and the fact that the party itself was going through a bit of an identity crisis. An examination of certain issues has begun. We are not changing our core beliefs as much as we are re-examining some issues again through our original lens of conservatism and seeing that we may have unintentionally come down on the wrong side of personal liberty. On other issues we need to stick to our guns... literally. In the case of gun control but also on illegal immigration. Any thought of deviating from our core beliefs simply to patronize a voting block must be vanquished immediately, besides it's not necessary for us to deviate. The Hispanic community wants to live in a nation of laws and among law-abiding people just as much as anyone else does.

Just as in 1986, we will have to come up with an acceptable compromise for those who can demonstrate they have already been living in our country, but this time adequate border control must be established and much more severe penalties must be imposed on those who feel they can willfully violate our laws by illegally entering the United States.

In addition to this updated focus, it is imperative that we take every opportunity to correct any historical inaccuracies and to explain and demonstrate our core conservative beliefs. If we are successful in articulating our positions of individual liberty and responsibility, a more limited and un-intrusive government, and equal opportunity for all, it will be much more difficult for our opponents to make false assertions about who we are and what we believe.

The outcomes of the elections of 2016 and 2020 will likely influence the better part of the first half of your life and beyond. Given the importance of these two elections, it is incredibly important that you understand the consequences, that you understand what is at stake, and that you have an accurate description of the two party platforms and their agendas. The consequences of these elections are too important to rely on what you think you know, you've heard, you have seen on the news and what you may have been taught in school. You must take it upon yourself and not simply fall into line with whatever demographic group you may find yourself in. You are a free-thinking individual. The consequences are too important. The success or failure of our country over the next twenty-five years all begins with you and your generation.